Dish

Published by

Princeton Architectural Press

37 East Seventh Street

New York, New York 10003

For a free catalog of books, call 1.800.722.6657.

Visit our web site at www.papress.com.

For Princeton Architectural Press

Editing: Clare Jacobson

Editorial assistance: Scott Tennent and Megan Carey

Design: Jan Haux

Special thanks to: Nettie Aljian, Nicola Bednarek, Janet Behning,

Penny (Yuen Pik) Chu, Russell Fernandez, John King, Mark

Lamster, Nancy Eklund Later, Linda Lee, Katharine Myers, Jane

Sheinman, Jennifer Thompson, Joseph Weston, and Deb Wood

—Kevin C. Lippert, publisher

The Dish exhibition is organized and circulated by Exhibitions

International, New York.

Project managing: Leah Goldberg Shandler and Osanna Urbay

Library of Congress Cataloging-in-Publication Data

Dish : international design for the home / Julie Müller Stahl, editor ;

foreword by Susan Yelavich.

    p. cm.

  Includes bibliographical references.

  ISBN 1-56898-476-6 (alk. paper)

  1. Women designers—Biography. 2. Women designers—

History—20th century. I. Stahl, Julie Müller.

  NK1174.D57 2005

  745.4'082'0904—dc22

                                                    2004008182

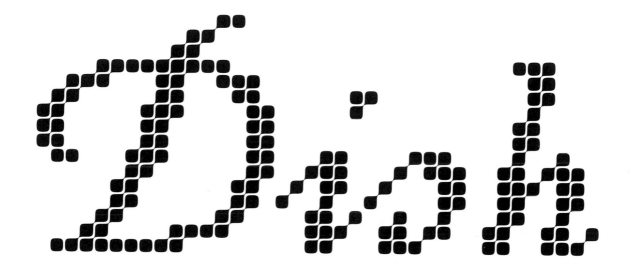

Dish

INTERNATIONAL DESIGN FOR THE HOME

Julie Müller Stahl, editor

Foreword by Susan Yelavich

Princeton Architectural Press, New York

CONTENTS

Foreword

WHAT'S THE DISH ON DESIGN?

Susan Yelavich

> **Dish** / *n* 1: a more or less concave vessel from
> which its contents, often food, are held and/or
> served 2: something that is favored 3. (slang)
> an attractive woman.

When Julie Müller Stahl first wrote me of her plans for
Dish, she included the definition above. My immediate
reaction was that the dictionary had missed something.
Namely, "dish" as dirt, gossip, or storytelling, as in, "What's
the dish on her?" And, on examining the work, I was
struck by how many of the designers were, in fact, engaged
in some form of narrative. Dishing it up, as it were.

Of course, the story of recent industrial design
has been the thawing of the object. Cold functionality
has been eschewed in favor of the pull of emotion. The
great anxiety about the increasingly expendable nature
of the things in our lives (particularly those things
digital) sent designers to the attic—the attic of design
above the space of modernism—looking for ideas that
would make their work as desirable as heirlooms past.
One could argue that a Pandora's box of design was
opened in service of a faceless binary code. However
that may be, the dish is…the story took another turn.

The new millennium has embraced the sensuality
of craft and materials on their own terms—not to sex
up the cell phone, the laptop, or the flat screen TV, all of
which have, at least temporarily, found their forms. We
have moved from the personalization of information tools
and toys to simply personalization. In some cases, the
user can customize and alter the product, as with Matali
Crasset's modular furniture and Ayse Birsel's Resolve
office system; in others, the persona privileged is the
designer herself, as in Laurene Leon Boym's Aphrodite
and Diana rugs and Ana Mir's Chocolate Nipples.

With the tether of functionality loosened, but not
untied, the designer is now also a curator, investigating
the particular nature of furnishings whose rich history
had long been ignored. What distinguishes the current
appetite for the past from the much-maligned excursions
of 1980s postmodernism is a sense of humor and
absence of grandiosity. Where the previous generation
looked to the authority of classicism, this one is drawn

to the subversive swing of the stylistic pendulum: the baroque, the mannered, and the vernacular. Nicolette Brunklaus's lamp shades draw freely from these idioms, as do Monica Nicoletti's Place Holders, cardboard boxes that become furniture by virtue of the "antique" images printed on them. While Brunklaus and Nicoletti play a game of inside out, Louise Campbell resolves the split identity between the reference and the object with her Between Two Chairs, transforming chairs into gargantuan handkerchiefs of lace. The merger of image and form takes on the surrealism of dreams in Sophie Demenge's Poulpa stool, whose legs reflect the arms of an octopus. Jessica Corr's Sir Donkey John Doe pillow was inspired by the futuristic scenarios of biotechnology, cushions of donkey heads are marked by random mutations built into the manufacturing process, itself a kind of cloning. Clearly, the not-so-unreal prospect of human replication has triggered another wave of ambivalence toward the machine and the machined in popular culture and, in turn, fueled the fires of the new iconoclasm in design.

Underneath the narratives and the critiques, underneath the tongue-in-cheek, pleasure of the pretty offered by all of these objects, lie more profound possibilities: the potency of beauty and prospect of a revitalized role for ornament. Beauty demands a physical response, a heightened sense of self in relationship to the object of desire, as with Inga Sempé's unabashedly romantic Grande Plissée Lampe and Dögg Gudmundsdottir's graceful Wing chair. Ornament is a code, a pattern, that unlocked yields beauty. Ornament need only be a fragile red thread running through a textile by Sarah Unruh. The strength of the attraction exerted by such a delicate gesture underscores how deeply we crave new optical intelligence.

To wit, beauty does not flow from a focus group, nor does invention. It comes from the confidence and craft of the designer. Likewise, the satisfaction we find in these pieces comes from discernment, not comparison-shopping. That the home should be the arena for these forays into personal narratives should not be surprising. This is the place where objects are rescued from commodity by dint of possession. Once possessed, a plate becomes the platform for *Dish*.

Susan Yelavich served as a juror and consultant for Dish. *She is an independent curator who writes about design and architecture. Yelavich is the author of* Contemporary World Interiors *(forthcoming in 2005),* Profile: Pentagram Design *(2004),* Design for Life *(1997), and* The Edge of the Millennium *(1993). She co-curated the 2003 National Design Triennial at the Cooper-Hewitt, National Design Museum. She is a Fellow of the American Academy in Rome.*

ACKNOWLEDGMENTS

Dish: International Design for the Home is the culmination
of the enormous dedication, time, energy, and talent
of the group of young women who first gathered together
to help organize its original incarnation, the exhibition
Transformation. Above all, a special acknowledgment
goes to Jessica Corr for her dedication and determination in initiating and bringing this project to fruition.
As co-curator of Transformation, and a designer herself,
she committed herself to all women working in the
industry. I would like to thank Parsons School of Design
and their exhibition staff for hosting the original exhibition; Mihako Koyama and Lora Lomiscio, whose insights
influenced the shaping of *Dish* and talents provided
the exhibit's exceptional lighting design; Alice Chung
and Karen Ting Hsu of Omnivore, Inc., for their intelligent
and striking graphic design; Lauren Macaulay, for being
creative with the bare necessities for the exhibition
design; and Annie Schlechter for her wonderful, photography. Without the crucial support of numerous other
individuals and institutions, the project's evolution into
Dish would not have been possible. In particular, I
would like to thank all the designers who shared their
work so openly and allowed me the opportunity to
explore what, where, and how women are designing.

The production of *Dish* relied on the keen interest and enthusiasm of both Clare Jacobson of
Princeton Architectural Press and Osanna Urbay of
Exhibitions International. Without their support, and the
support of their organizations and staffs, *Dish* would
never have come to be.

At Princeton Architectural Press, I am grateful to
Clare Jacobson, editorial director, for guiding me
through an unknown process with boundless patience—
especially when it came to receiving the unexpected—
and for her thorough editing and high standards; and
to Jan Haux for his keen understanding and graphic
design sensibility throughout *Dish*. At Exhibitions
International I would like to give additional gratitude to
Robert T. Buck, David Shearer, Kate Clark, Dorys
Codina, and Leah Goldberg Shandler.

A very special thanks goes to each of the
distinguished essayists who shared their unique
perspectives: Hazel Clark, Johanna Grawunder, Pat
Kirkham, Julie Lasky, and Patrizia Moroso. I am

especially indebted to Susan Yelavich, not only for her valuable participation as a juror and writer for *Dish* but also for her encouragement to launch the exhibition on a tour. She has been an astute and sound presence for me throughout the project. I am also grateful to Chee Pearlman for her generous involvement as a juror.

Other collaborators who deserve recognition: Myung Choi of Bartok Design for creating a wonderful website; Tim Valdez at Crozier Fine Arts for carefully overseeing the storage of all the works; Barrie Olsen for her skilled and timely editorial support; Sandra Heins for her indispensable assistance with the enormity of detail; and my family for their understanding and support. Finally, I thank Joseph Calabrese, without whose continuous support and unshakable confidence in me I would never have endured this project.

Introduction

DESIGN: THE ART OF THE MOMENT

Julie Müller Stahl

In December 2001, I received an email from Jessica
Corr about organizing an exhibition to promote women
in the field of industrial design. We had each experienced walking through major design events confounded
by the often total absence of women, albeit uninten-
tional (no one had an exhibit entitled Men in Design).
And we knew that although women represent roughly
half of the student body enrolled in art and design
schools today, their work is overshadowed by that of
their counterparts. As a designer herself, Jessica knew
a number of women who were doing very interesting,
cutting-edge work, not unlike her own. However, the
work was underground, undiscovered. It needed to be
brought into the public's eye. Thus, the seed for Dish,

originally organized as the exhibit Transformation,
was planted

We sought out pieces that were innovative in
regards to their fabrication, material, or concept, designs
rarely published or exhibited from both emerging and
established designers internationally. During our
research, we noticed a prevailing sensorial nature in the
work; it was personal, narrative, witty, conceptual,
sensuous, responsive, and unrestrained. We decided to
focus on home products, not because the domestic
realm has always been considered women's territory, but
because the home is where design can be expressive
and uninhibited. In addition, objects found in the
home have a historical and cross-cultural precedence
that newer products, such as computers, do not.

When Transformation opened in June 2003 at
Parsons School of Design people sensed a cohesive
sensibility to the work. The exhibition crystallized the
essence of what was happening in design on the whole.
Some viewers recognized the gender behind it, while
others did not—and that is just as well. What they saw
was the work alone. Regardless of the gender of
the designer, personalization in design has permeated
the industry. Form no longer follows function but
emotion, although function is no less important.[1] When
Ayse Birsel designed her award-winning Resolve office
system for Herman Miller in 1999, she reinvented the
standard in office design breaking through long-accepted

ideas of what defined an office—traditionally, men's territory. The Resolve system offers flexibility, customization, and personalization, which celebrate the uniqueness of each individual. In retrospect, its success prophesied these characteristics as the driving force in the future of design. Such traits are consistent throughout *Dish*, and, while not exclusive to women, they are often seen or described as innately feminine.

The majority of work by women designers, particularly those based in the United States, is self-produced and, therefore, seldom seen. Manufacturers, producers, and distributors represent few women. Consequently, galleries, stores, design books, and trade magazines often overlook the work of many talented female designers. But perhaps the answer to this imbalance no longer lies in whether women are receiving equal attention and recognition, but rather how women are approaching a career in this industry. After meeting with women designers over the last two years, I have come to understand that their lives are far from those of typical, independent, male designers—particularly if they have children. Their identities do not revolve solely around being "a designer." They take on many roles: mother, wife, daughter, designer, entrepreneur, artist, lover, friend, activist, writer, and teacher. It is a struggle to balance the time between these roles, but, as Lyn Godley asserts, "My definition of myself [is] far broader than a lot of male designers I know. My whole identity is not wrapped up in being successful in one specific thing and, therefore, not so critical. In fact, I believe this multifaceted life most women have results in bringing a fuller sense of life to their design work."[2]

Women have an intrinsic ability to transform, to change, and to carry many roles simultaneously. Traditionally they do not follow a straight and narrow path. None of the women represented in *Dish* are dogmatic in their design approach. There is a tendency in the work to combine varying and sometimes opposing elements, such as design with fashion, craft with high technology, and functionality with narrative, resulting in an intriguing layering or complexity. For many women, the most fulfilling aspect of design is generating an emotional connection between the user and the object. The *Dish* designers challenge convention, push the boundaries of design, and shock us with the unexpected.

The understanding and appreciation of aesthetic value in product design is increasing throughout popular culture and mass industries alike, with magazines such as *Time* and *BusinessWeek* devoting entire issues to the subject. Consumers have never had so much choice in every product at any price point. They are forced to decide what they really like, what defines them and expresses their personalities, in much the same way they choose the clothes they wear. "Industrial design," a term formerly reserved for power-driven (and thus "masculine") machinery, now pertains to a variety of systems. Technology has played a large part in this change, allowing design to go beyond mass production and into mass customization and so shifting design from a strong masculine sensibility based upon rationality and efficiency to a feminine one of individualism and sensorial beauty.

I hope the collection of work presented in *Dish* will expand people's perspectives of women in the industry, acknowledging the various paths they take. The work reinforces that "masculine" and "feminine" only define divergent sensibilities that are often blended and do not necessarily mirror the gender of the designer. *Dish* is not only a collection of unique and varied work from women throughout the world, but also a testament to the strength of their individual voices. In the end, I hope manufacturers, writers, and consumers will have the courage to embrace these voices more readily, recognizing their power and potential.

The *Dish* designers have gone beyond years of preconceived ideas to communicate their own experi-ence and perception of life. They have spoken out while much has been unspoken, and so we can expect that they will bring even more innovations grounded in social, cultural, and emotional realms. At the beginning of the twenty-first century, industrial design is one of the fastest growing professions. Women are finding them-selves with a lot of choices and a lot of questions that have not been asked. This is a time of transition and

transformation. Let us hope that *Dish's* efforts to communicate the uncommunicated will bring inspiration, recognition, and support of the design community and beyond.

1   Hartmut Esslinger, cited in Owen Edwards, "Form Follows Emotion," *Forbes ASAP* 29 November 1999, 237–8.

2   Lyn Godley, e-mail message to author, September 29, 2003.

Julie Müller Stahl is the founder of her eponymous firm that is a conduit between industry and contemporary design. She is an independent curator and handles a combination of strategic design relations, creative marketing, and public relations. She lives in New York.

The Dish from a Historian

GENDERING DESIGN 1900–2000

Pat Kirkham

American women designers are now visible in every
area of the field, from industrial to interior design, and
from graphic to landscape design. The changes that led
women to find spaces and places to work in the design
professions over the last hundred years were part of
broader historical changes predicated in part upon
new ideas about what was appropriate for women to
think and do. The "male sphere" of paid work and public
presence, as opposed to the more private "female
sphere" of domesticity, was increasingly encroached
upon by women.[1] As in other areas of paid work, the
major leaps forward in education and training, as well
as entry into hitherto proscribed occupations, coincided
with the two main periods of concerted feminist

activism: the women's emancipation movement of the
late nineteenth and early twentieth centuries and
the women's liberation movement from the late 1960s
to the 1980s—and beyond, for many of us.

In a major research project, *Women Designers in
the USA, 1900–2000: Diversity and Difference,* most
of the issues raised by the designers in *Dish* surfaced.[2]
Women in the study exhibited a great diversity of both
routes to becoming a designer and modes of practicing
as one, as well as enormous differences in the ways
they experienced and articulated being a designer. *Dish*
confirms that considerations of diversity and difference
as well as commonalities continue to be central to dis-
cussions about the practices of women designers today.
An obvious but often forgotten point is that gender cannot be considered in isolation. It continually intersects in
all manner of ways with factors such as ethnicity, class,
region, education and training, parental and familial
influence (many of the women who trained as industrial
designers had some form of hands-on practical
experience at home), mentoring, age, contacts, views
of marriage and motherhood, personal and economic
circumstances, and, of course, sheer talent.

Today women dominate the fields of interior
design, fashion, jewelry, and textiles, accounting for over
eighty percent of practitioners, while in other fields, such
as ceramics and graphics, they account for half of those
employed as designers. Not surprisingly, the area of

design that most eschewed decoration and was most closely associated with engineering and technology—industrial design—proved the most resistant to women entering its ranks. Today women account for only about twenty percent of the profession, and that has only been achieved in the last decade. Many design fields continue to show "an appalling lack of ethnic diversity."[3] Women of color are few and far between not only in industrial design but also in fields in which women predominate, including interior design and film costume design. Interestingly, they have fared much better in graphic design, an area that only began to accept women in any significant numbers in the 1970s, a decade when ethnicity and gender issues were widely and simultaneously challenged in the United States.

Women are now part of every design profession, but their entry into different areas was uneven, to say the least. It was easiest in areas deemed feminine through association with decoration, domestic culture, and amateur practices. In 1900—with the exception of embroidery, the decoration of china, and some other "crafts" carried out mainly in the home or small workshops—professional design was exclusively a male domain. Jewelry, metalwork and interior design were beginning to open up to women because, like embroidery and other decorative work, they were deemed sufficiently feminine for respectable women to work in them. Notions of appropriate behavior remained largely defined by the nineteenth-century cult of domesticity and "true womanhood," which depicted women as genteel guardian angels of home, taste, and morality.[4]

Although areas such as interior design (or interior decorating, as it was then called), decorative ceramics, and jewelry could be defined as "feminine," the very idea of women entering them led to deep anxieties on the part of some men. Such were fears of effeminacy that, when Elsie de Wolfe declared interior decorating a feminine pursuit in *The House in Good Taste* (1913), Frank Parsons (after whom the famous New York design school is named) immediately reclaimed it as masculine.[5]

In general, women who wanted to design large-scale or "hard" products—including furniture, washing machines, public gardens and landscapes, or sets for movies—had the hardest time breaking down gender barriers. In the first half of the century in particular, women tended to work on smaller items, regardless of field. The strength necessary to make certain objects was cited as a reason for excluding women from designing them, although, of course, the act of designing does not rely upon strength. One has to remember that there is rarely (if ever) any rationality in the so-called rationales that seek to naturalize gender divisions of labor. Strength and dirt, together with size, encoded the masculine within dominant cultural discourses. Arguments about the tough and dirty nature of construction, together with the notion that women would not be able to handle construction crews, also applied to architecture and landscape architecture. However, women broke into those occupations at the turn of the century.

Issues of strength and size also operate within furniture design, where women rarely strayed beyond decorative carving and making small domestic items until the 1970s. Today, women such as Judy Kensley McKie, Kristina Madsen, Rosanne Summerson, Cheryl Riley, and Wendy Maruyama are well known as designers of high-quality postmodern studio furniture, some of which incorporate issues of femininity and feminism. Several of them make their own pieces, cutting across stereotypes of woodworkers as men, just as Eva Zeisel (a ceramist and industrial designer) cuts across stereotypes of a 98-year-old grandmother by working as a top-level designer.

One of the most striking things about gender divisions *within* particular design fields during the last century was that women tended to work on interior, domestic projects. In interior design, women tended to focus on domestic projects; indeed, so close was (and is) the popular association of women with interior design that it is often seen to come "naturally" to them. Lucia DeRespinis, who was trained as an industrial designer, claims that whenever interiors were part of a project at the design office headed by George Nelson in the 1950s, she was assigned to them: "It was because I was

a woman, and women were supposed to be naturally good at interior design."[6] Even in landscape design, where spaces were not interior, women tended to work on garden design for domestic residences. Such gendered allocations of work were strongest during the first half of the century, but many were only seriously challenged in the 1970s and 1980s.

Automobiles are well outside the realm of domestic interiority, but when women designers first found work in the automobile industry in the 1930s and 1940s, their efforts were restricted to the interiors of family vehicles. General Motors hired women designers for their "feminine sensibilities" in an attempt to give automobile interiors "woman appeal."[7] Suzanne Vanderbilt was one such "damsel of design." Although she remained with the company for twenty-three years, was promoted to chief designer of Chevrolet interiors, and designed interiors for tractors and small trucks, GM never gave her the opportunity to design an automobile body, despite the high caliber of her work.[8] Today transportation design is the most gendered area within the design professions; it has the distinction of having fewer women students than any other area of design in the United States.[9]

Most of the issues that contemporary women designers face in juggling demands upon their time—including childcare, interrupted career patterns, working with a spouse or significant other, and "glass ceilings"—

were issues throughout the past century. Oppositions such as private versus public, and personal versus work-related, can only hint at the real situations and sacrifices faced by some women over the century, particularly when they were the main economic supporter of a family. Indeed, certain women now famous in their fields, such as garden designer Ellen Biddle Shipman, began to work professionally only when they found themselves on their own with children to support. Others worked from home when they had children, often abandoning their preferred area of work for one that was more accommodating to their new situation. Some found it easier to cope by working with their husbands, but until the 1970s (and, in many cases, beyond) it was generally the women within "designer couples" who bore the brunt of domestic responsibilities. Ray Eames was something of an exception among women designers in the third quarter of the century in that she did not have the responsibilities of children and a cook was employed at the design office where she and her husband, Charles Eames, spent much of their time.[10]

Dish and other recent exhibitions about women designers suggest that something is happening over and above the sheer pleasure in seeing excellent work that happens to be by women.[11] It is difficult to define precisely what that something is, but large numbers of women (and not a few men) viewers have used the terms "uplifting," "inspiring," "moving," and "reaffirming" after seeing work of consistently high standards by women designers. This suggests that, like the women who argued tactically for a separate exhibition of women's art and design at the 1893 World's Columbian Exposition in Chicago in order to better highlight women's achievements, the organizers of this book and exhibition were right to highlight work by women. Let us hope that this will lead to a better understanding of the products and experiences of women designers at the beginning of the twenty-first century.

1   Among European Americans, it was mainly "respectable" middle-class women who became professional designers. Working-class women had always worked—even during the nineteenth century when notions of women as guardians of the home, taste, and morality were at their strongest. For an overview of American women in the twentieth century see Eileen Boris's chapter "Social Change and Changing Experience" in Pat Kirkham, ed., *Women Designers in the USA, 1900–2000: Diversity and Difference* (London: Yale University Press, 2000), 36–47, and the timeline on the preceding ten pages. For women as guardians of hearth and home see note 4 below.

2   Substantive parts of this essay are taken from Kirkham, *Women Designers*. I would like to take this opportunity to thank again all those historians, curators, and designers who worked on that enormous project between 1997 and 2000.

3 Pat Kirkham and Lynne Walker, "Women Designers in the USA, 1900–2000: Diversity and Difference," in Kirkham, *Women Designers*, 74.

4 See B. Welter, "The Cult of True Womanhood 1820–1860," *American Quarterly* 18 (1966): 151–74; Penny Sparke, *As Long as It's Pink: The Sexual Politics of Taste* (London. Pandora, 1995), 15–72; and Pat Kirkham and Penny Sparke, "'A Woman's Place…' Women Interior Designers," in Kirkham, *Women Designers*, 304–16.

5 See Peter McNeil, "Designing Women: Gender, Sexuality and the Interior Decorator, c. 1890–1940," *Art History* 17 (1994): 631–57. Parsons headed an onslaught against untrained yet talented women who dared to enter an occupation he wanted reserved for those with paper qualifications and standardized training.

6 Lucia DeRespinis, conversation with author, 1999. See also Ella Howard and Eric Setliff, "'In a Man's World': Women Industrial Designers," in Kirkham, *Women Designers*, 284–5.

7 Howard and Setliff, "'In a Man's World,' " 282–4.

8 Ibid., 284–5, and Kirkham and Walker, "Women Designers," 64–5.

9 Kirkham and Walker, "Women Designers," 74.

10 See Pat Kirkham, *Charles and Ray Eames: Designers of the Twentieth Century* (Cambridge, Mass.: MIT Press, 1995). Husband-wife partnerships were a relatively new but distinctive feature of design practice in the United States in the 1940s and reflected new, more mutually respectful, modes of "companionate" marriage. See Virginia Wright Wexman, *Creating the Couple: Love, Marriage, and Hollywood Performance* (Princeton: Princeton University Press, 1993).

11 See, for example, *Goddess in the Details: Product Design by Women*, organized by the Association of Women Industrial Designers and the Department of Exhibitions at Pratt Institute, Brooklyn, 1994.

Pat Kirkham is a professor in the history of design, decorative arts, and culture at the Bard Graduate Center, New York. She is well known for her work in design history, women's studies, and film studies. She is the editor of numerous books including Women Designers in the USA, 1900–2000: Diversity and Difference, The Gendered Object, Charles and Ray Eames: Designers of the Twentieth Century, *and* A View from the Interior: Women and Design *(edited with Judy Attfield).*

1

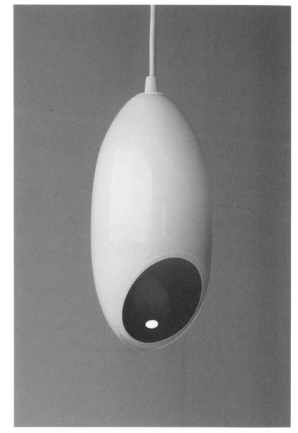

2

Lindsey Adams Adelman

Butter

Born:
New York, USA

Practice:
New York, USA

Growing up, I was drawn to the patterns of Marimekko sheets, Heller bowls, Danskin striped outfits, and my family's Ericofon without being specifically aware of design with a capital "D." My interests gravitated toward computers and the fine arts until I met an industrial designer who was creating French fries out of foam for a Smithsonian exhibition. I thought, "What a way to make a living." I applied to Rhode Island School of Design, and my life has not been the same.

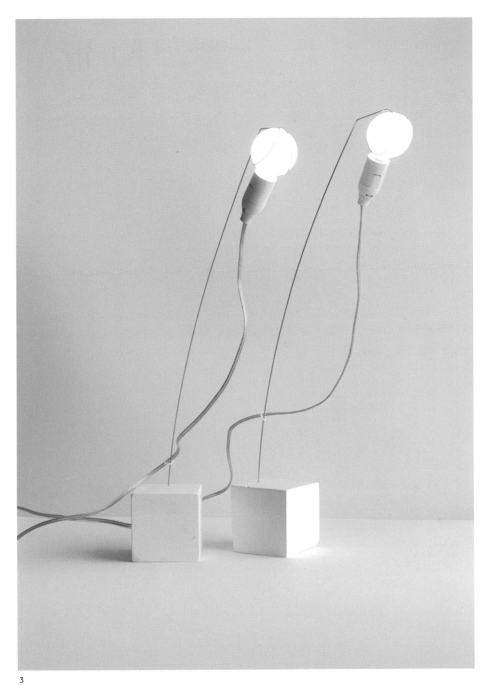

1. Study for "Exercise for Girls" video, 2003. Gouache on paper.

2. Venus pendant light, 2002. Hand-blown glass, electrical parts. Designed with Suzanne Charbonnet.

3. One-Bulb table light, 2003. Concrete, steel wire, electrical parts. Designed by Butter.

3

What I do for my job and what I do with my free time are not really that different. Making is what I do. I am motivated when I cannot find the exact thing I have in mind, whether a light fixture, bag, or queen-size bed with storage underneath. *When you begin to learn how things are made, you can customize your world.*

Although I formerly designed mass production pieces to provide accessibility, what interests me now is working with my hands and getting back to discovering forms through material manipulation. Such end products fall closer to art than design, as each piece is labor-intensive and unique. Being able to move between the worlds of mass and singular production is the ideal.

My work is inspired by a simple manipulation of material, as well as a specific function. I love working on lighting because it transforms space in a direct way. Products for the home will keep evolving as new materials are developed. The way we acquire

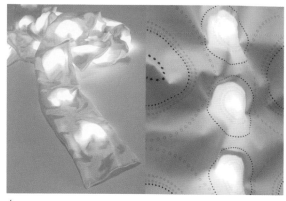

4

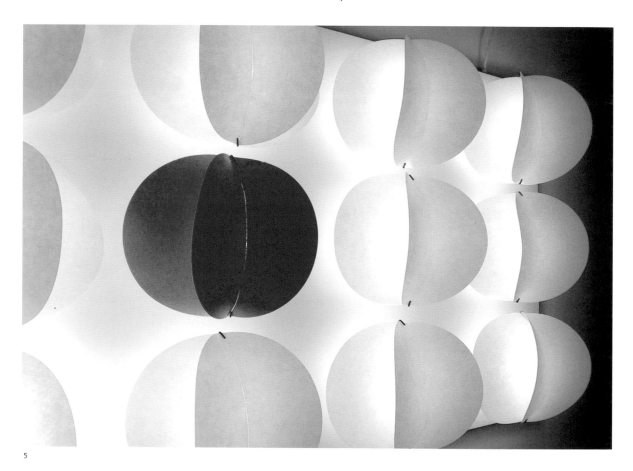

5

products is changing—it is so much easier to source things online and have them shipped direct.

As designers, women have an advantage when designing for female consumers and even children: we can address not-so-obvious details, functions, scale, color, form, and performance in ways that may not be apparent to male designers. As women are often more sensitive to these environments, this can translate into demanding fairer conditions for production. I have found a communal atmosphere among women

designers. There seems to be room for collaboration. Although we are still competitive, women are likely to help and work though ideas or problems. Lately I have been collaborating with Gigi Scandinaro and Keira Alexandra for Fake Company. Our projects balance humor with integrity.

I still believe in simple, high-quality designs at an affordable price. More than ever, the life cycle of a product needs to be taken into consideration. Anything that is put into production needs to be seriously

4. Soft knotted, hanging, or table light, 2003. Flame-resistant, fiberglass fabric, electrical parts. Designed by Butter.

5. Lunette clip-on shade, 2000. Fiberglass paper, steel clip. Designed by Butter.

6. Light in Pieces, 2003. Maple veneer with polycarbonate laminate, electrical parts.

6

considered in terms of longevity—what happens when the life of the product is over? Is this something we really need? And what aspects can be improved upon from a sustainable design viewpoint?

I hope I inspire others to make their own products, and that they will follow their intuition and make things rather than only buying them, use what they have in new ways, and shape their spaces to be exactly how they want them rather than the way they think they are supposed to be.

1

1. Good Egg footstool, 1996. Post-consumer egg crates.

2. Lotus sitting rug, 2000. Wool rug, canvas backing, plastic inserts.

3. Stone pillows, 2000. Buckwheat hulls, Lycra.

Inna Alesina
Alesina Design

Born:
Kharkov, Ukraine

Practice:
Baltimore, USA

I became a designer by a lucky accident. The school to which I was applying (back in Soviet Union) was accepting more students for its industrial design program than for any other. So I decided to enroll and later transfer to something more "artistic." But as soon as I learned what industrial design actually was, I never wanted to do anything else. Working in three dimensions and solving real problems to improve people's circumstances is very interesting and inspiring.

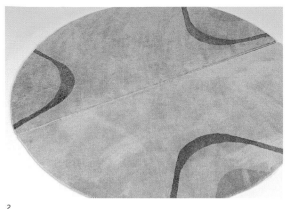

2

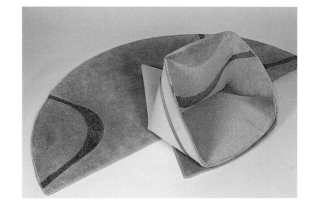

3

The biggest challenge that industrial designers face is that we do not realize how much power we actually have. We can make a real difference in people's lives, and we are responsible for the environmental impact of our design decisions. But most people still think that design is about making pretty shapes. I think it will take time and effort to educate people that the beauty of an object is in the way it solves a problem. If this is achieved in a minimal way, all the better; I call this "elegant functionality." If I could, I would substitute the word "beautiful" with "logical," because beauty is subjective, but design is not.

The idea behind the object is very important to me. I like objects that have meanings on many levels and make references to many areas of our lives. I like multifunctional or transformable objects and try to make things more than what they seem at the first glance. I like my designs to tell a story. Some of my designs come from what I call "passive inspiration," a found object that makes me think, "Cool! What could I do

4

4. Brick bag, 2000. Prototype made of paper, cardboard, fabric, industrial cable.

5. Nesting menorah, 2003. Aluminum.

6. Straw lamp, 1999. Drinking straws, soda bottle, electrical parts.

with that?" But when I have a problem to solve, the inspiration is no longer passive, and I know the best solution needs to be found. Then the question is, "What is the best way to achieve that?"

Industrial designers can look to changes in lifestyles in order to find new problems to solve. I think that space (or, rather, the lack of it) will be one of the biggest problems in the future, so objects will have to be either multifunctional or out of sight between uses. New materials and technology will change every-

thing around us. Hopefully we will be making things sustainable and think of new sources of energy and resources.

I would say that design is actually the oldest profession (despite the common joke). When the first humans shaped a rock to make the first tool, they were solving a problem. It took generations to improve the design. We have better tools now and our processes are faster, but the same rule still applies: the designer has

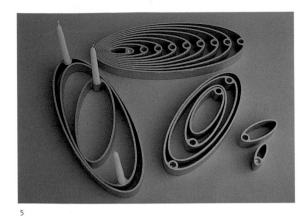

5

6

to be a user. So when people say, "Everything has been done a long time ago. What is there new to design?" my answer is that there are still real problems to be solved. We should design products that have real purpose and improve lives because we have the power and tools to do so and because we have something else, we have a passion to create.

1. Red Snapper desk set, 2001. Polypropylene, steel tubing, plastic laminate. Produced by Herman Miller.

2. Red Rocket desk set with file cart, 2001. Particle board with melamine surface, PVC, steel tubing, injection molded glass-filled nylon, steel, Dupont Cordura, vinyl, nylon mesh, elastic cord, ABS plastic, urethane. Produced by Herman Miller.

Ayse Birsel
Olive 1:1

Born:
Izmir, Turkey

Practice:
New York, USA and Paris, France

The intimacy, three-dimensionality, and human scale of industrial design led me to choose it over architecture and urban design. My definition of industrial design is exactly what the two words imply: industry and design coming together. Industry brings the knowledge, experience, and know-how of engineers, researchers, marketers, and fabricators. Design brings my outsider's eye, creativity, and the freedom to imagine. Together we solve problems and bring products to market.

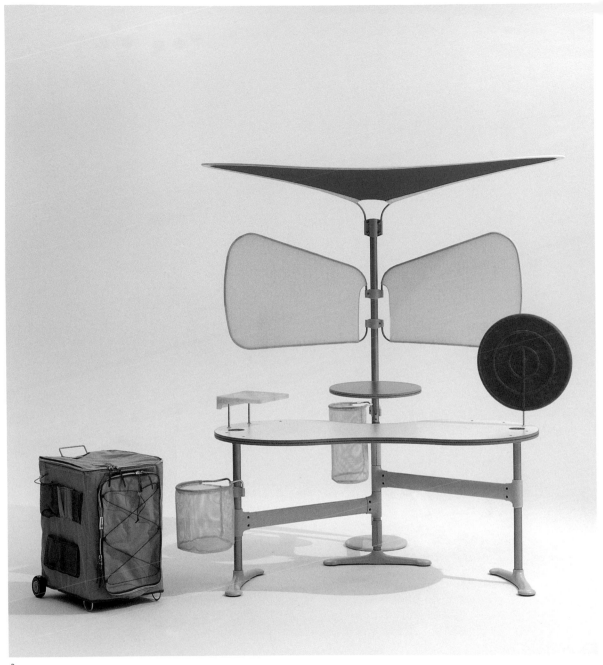

2

My best work is with large manufacturers on mass-
manufactured products for mass markets. In approaching design, I think for the user. Hence, my work is
user-centered and solution-oriented. *Inspiration
comes from watching people until
you see what can be instead of what
has been.* In order to arrive at a better solution
you need to break with age-old, accepted conventions.

Being a woman defines my gender. Being
a designer defines my profession. One does not bring

an advantage to the other. In my work, I strive to
communicate that good design can enhance your
everyday life.

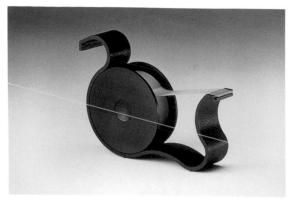

3

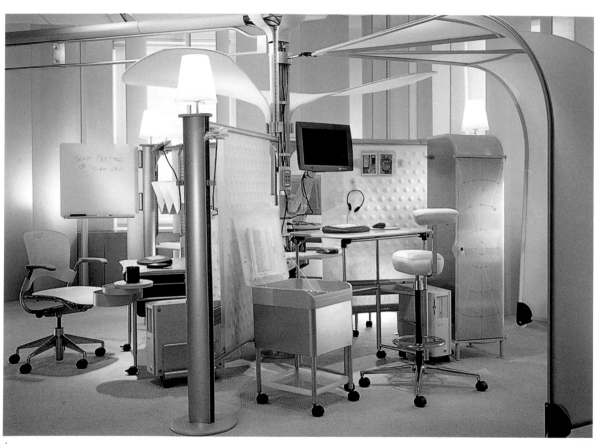

4

3. Orchestra tape dispenser, 1991.
ABS plastic. Designed by
Hannah/Birsel. Produced by Knoll.

4. Resolve office system, 2000.
Powder-coated steel, plastic, coated
MDF, proprietary display fabrics.
Produced by Herman Miller.

5. Oscar towels, 2000. Cotton.
Produced by Merati.

6. Tulip bath accessories, 2001.
Ceramic and metal. Produced by
Decorum.

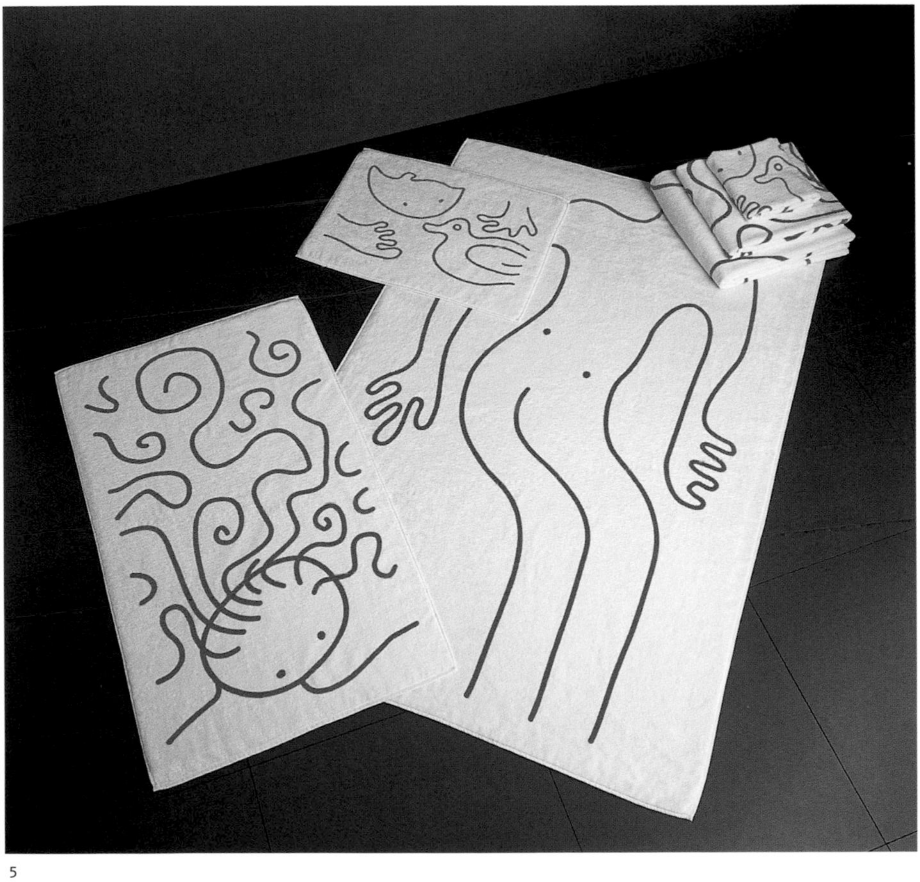

5

6

7. Oscar light and shelf, tooth-brush cone, and soap dispenser, 2000. Molded, abrasion-resistant Methacrylate plastic. Produced by Merati.

8. Oscar sink system, 2000. Methacrylate plastic. Produced by Merati.

5. She coffee table, 2001. Steel tube base, soft-formed MDF or walnut top. Designed by Johanna Egnell. Produced by David Design.

3. Children's plate and mug, 2003. Plastic. Produced by IKEA.

4. Children's cutlery, 2003. Plastic. Designed by Johanna Egnell. Produced by IKEA.

1. Clic sofa, 2002. Steel frame, molded polyurethane seat in molded cold-cured polyester and fiber, chrome legs. Produced by Söderbergs.

2. Sittcarpet, 2002. Felt. Designed by Helena Bodin.

1

2

Helena Bodin & Johanna Egnell

bodinegnell

Born:
Stockholm, Sweden

Practice:
Stockholm, Sweden

Designers work creatively with materials to give form to products in order to realize the optimal environment. As designers, we refer to the present to discover new and innovative ways to communicate and connect with people. Yet history inspires us as well. Whatever the product, it must be designed for its purpose and thought through well.

We work with self-production and large manufacturers. With self-production, we do not have to compromise the form and quality of our designs so our ideas usually go further. Nevertheless, disadvantages

3

4

5

lie in the economic challenges and hard work entailed in marketing your products. With a large manufacturer, such as IKEA, we can design products in plastic, which requires expensive tools for molding. It is extremely rewarding to work with skilled product developers and manufacturers. There is the added benefit of their marketing and public relations capabilities, which give us greater exposure. *The challenge in design is to always go one more step, to be critical and recognize when a design is not good or needs further refinement.* In seeking a solution to a problem, we try a lot of ideas and are very observant, finding inspiration in a multitude of things. Design is personal and ever changing. Inventions change the way we approach situations and, as a consequence, create a need for products suited for a new way of life.

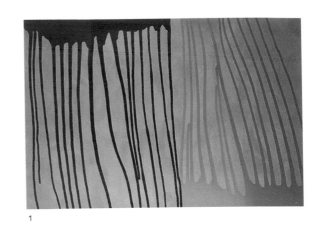

1

2

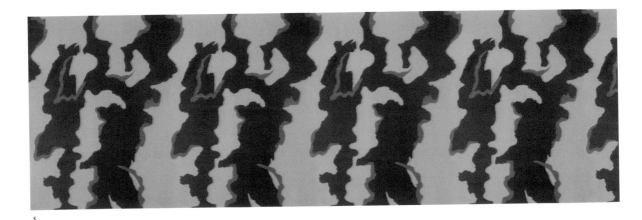

3

Kelly Bortoluzzi & Kristin Oidahl

Orbo Design

Born:
Milwaukee, USA (KB), New York, USA (KO)

Practice:
New York, USA

We both share a passion for textile design, as well as the creative freedom of painting. By making painted rugs we realized we could have the best of both worlds: the scope and fluidity of painting along with the function and discipline of design. As a result, we created a product that surpassed its colonial origins in both look and feel.

The idea began when Kristin, an artist, started turning paintings into canvas rugs to cover the floor of her loft. Kelly, a product designer, was intrigued by the painterly rugs. We collaborated on one for a mutual

1. Warm Spills rug, 2002. Hand-painted canvas.

2. Cool Bands runner, 2002. Hand-painted canvas.

3. Camouflage for Peace, Fabmat floor mat, 2003. Waterproof nylon canvas.

4. Custom Circles rug, 2000. Hand-painted canvas. Produced for DB House by Fink and Platt Architects.

4

friend's wedding present. We enjoyed the process and result so much that we decided to found Orbo Design.

What we found most exciting about starting our business was the initial product development. We turned our studio into a test lab for formulas, techniques, and production procedures, setting out to not only give the traditional floor cloth a fresh look, but to also significantly improve on the form's surface quality and durability.

With their bold colors and designs that referred to abstract painting, our revamped floor coverings caught the eye of collectors, architects, and the media. *Custom work was rolling in, but we were also interested in developing a more affordable, mass-producible item* with similar properties to the canvas rug. Finding a manufacturer who was willing to experiment with small runs and new techniques proved very tricky. Eventually, the Fabmat—a mass-produced, waterproof, nylon-canvas floor mat—was born! To now be in the position where we can grow beyond our studio is very exciting.

1

𝓛𝒶𝓊𝓇𝒾𝑒𝓃𝑒 𝓛𝑒𝑜𝓃
𝓑𝑜𝓎𝓂

𝓑𝑜𝓎𝓂 𝓟𝒶𝓇𝓉𝓃𝑒𝓇𝓈

Born:
New York, USA

Practice:
New York, USA

My entry into design, when I was in my early twenties, was conditioned by an accidental event. Retrospectively, it was kismet. I helped my then-boyfriend Constantin Boym design an "edible pencil" for an IDSA (Industrial Designers Society of America) competition. He developed the concept, I developed the form and baked it in the oven— it was made of cookie dough and graphite. Imagine my shock when we won first place! The project caught the public's imagination, and both of us were quickly caught up in a media feeding frenzy. Looking back on it,

2

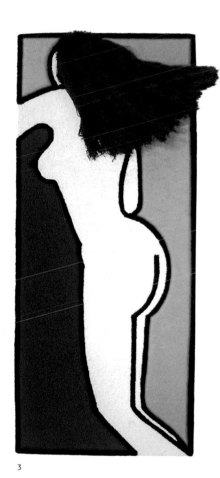

3

I was incredibly lucky to have such a positive introduction to the design world. I was seduced by it, in fact.

The work we do at Boym Partners, both client-driven and self-produced, comes from a place of enlightenment and experience. Our practice addresses questions that we as human beings need answered. Some of our designs manifest themselves as mirrors to particular cultural conditions or events; many derive from a known psychological need; some are simply objects we imagine and would like in our house. Since I started collaborating with Constantin, we have experimented with a literary approach in product direction, development, and manufacturing. The work is content-driven and methodical. On the other hand, I am entrenched in American pop culture and direct my design responses to a level of visual cues that appear in other cultural media.

In our work with large-scale manufacturers I rely on my client and/or editors to help me make the right choice of project direction and development.

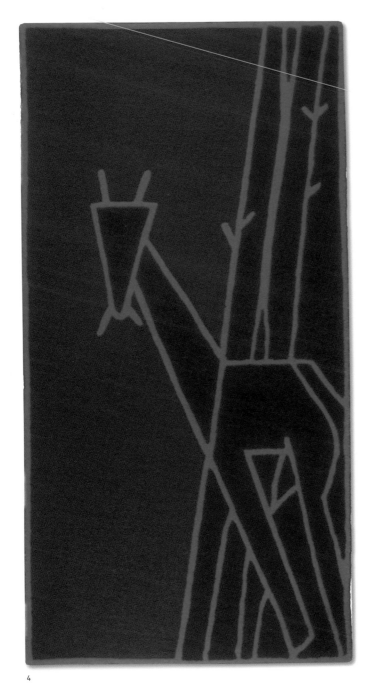

We also practice self-production, and regard it as the laboratory for experimentation. Small production runs or unique objects are petri dishes for an idea, an object, and an environment. We use rapid prototyping and digital craft to streamline the process. *The best possible manifestation occurs when the freshness and experimentation of self-generated work partners with the experience and infrastructure of well-known manufacturers.*

In the near future, there will be more and more of a blurring of these two modes of making objects. The smartest and most sophisticated manufacturers are already issuing specially designed, limited-edition products.

Now, we see a return to the decorated object and a sense of whimsy in product design. Coming up are design objects that reference fashion, music, film, and so on. More and more, the vanguard of consumer products and furnishings for the home are

5

6

becoming a cultural vortex. It is a very exciting time
for designers on the frontlines, because they have a lot
of material with which to play.

1

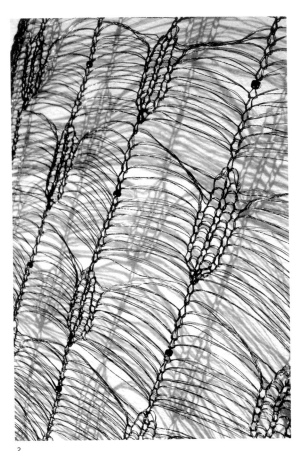

2

Diana Brennan

I am fascinated by the constructive and sensory awareness that the textile medium imparts. It offers structural,
conceptual, and sensuous questions that create
an enriching area of study. What is it made from? Which
materials have been used? What sensations do these
combinations of information trigger? It is this alchemy to
which I react.

*I like to push the boundaries of
design by bringing unconventional
materials into products for the home,*

Born:
Sydney, Australia

Practice:
Paris, France

1. The Alchemist's Means, 2003. Copper wire, nylon threads.

2. Pathway Shadows, 2003. Copper threads, Linea lineapui ramino yarn.

3. Entwined Pathways 1 and 2, 2003. Copper threads, glass beads.

3

where certain objects can have a dual purpose. They can be considered as functional, participating in their surrounding environment, and at the same time be viewed as an alternative art form that induces a sense of well-being.

I feel an affinity for media such as copper, stainless steel, and nylon threads. Part of my inspiration comes from the aesthetic and structural qualities of these industrially manufactured materials and the poetry that radiates from them. Copper threads are supple enough to be manipulated by hand. Although contact with metal is cold, it possesses seductive, visual qualities.

Large surfaces made from such lightweight, high-strength materials can be easily transported and hung. The shiny quality of the metallic threads assimilates light, making it an active element of the work. Backlighting accentuates the structural and graphic aspect of open-worked patterns. When the light source is reoriented or when the spectator moves, the lace motif dissolves into a scintillating surface of

4

5

metallic threads that capture and refract the light. This allows for a certain kind of fantasy not found in large-scale manufactured textiles.

One of my fundamental queries is, "How can I utilize manufacturing techniques and industrial materials to enrich my forms and improve my working methods?" I work with a machine employed by the knitwear industry, but I use it to create one-off or very limited series production objects where each work has its individual identity. I work alone and undertake the whole production process myself, diverting materials from their original context and using them in a way in which they were not designed. Although this process is slow and contributes to the high production cost of each object, working manually with machines allows me a great deal of freedom to experiment with ideas.

6

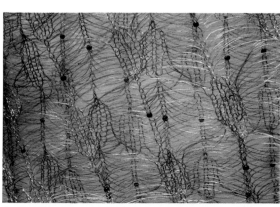

7

1

Nicolette Brunklaus

Nicolette Brunklaus Amsterdam

Born:
Eindoven, The Netherlands

Practice:
Amsterdam, The Netherlands

It is a challenge to find and maintain the balance between creating something poetic and something commercial. I was educated as an artist. My big change in direction came in 1993, when I started a collaboration with artist Lynne Leegte. We made a furniture collection, and I really enjoyed creating a series of works instead of one-off pieces.

The inspiration for my designs comes from imagery, scenes, and stories. After I establish the

2

3

initial idea, I search for the form and material to relate it. Not only is the quality of the object vital, but also its place as a piece of art that enhances the surrounding space.

Being a self-producing designer gives me freedom in how, when, and in what scale I produce a piece. This makes it possible to test the market with small quantities, so I do not have to make concessions. In 1998 I withdrew my products from wholesale companies and started selling my designs under the name "Nicolette Brunklaus Amsterdam." I began to retail via mail order, which grew into selling wholesale and to a national and international market.

Nevertheless, I keep my work personal instead of conforming it to a large audience. One personal exploration involved printed text. I had observed that text in designs was being used primarily for decoration. Instead, I used it as a invitation for users to communicate, sometimes quite literally; one of my products was a set of pillowcases with "yes" printed on one

4

5

side and "no" on the other. In my recent work, I use images as my language instead of text—the communication is on another level.

When I think about interior products in the future, I think about how globalization influences the shop collections, the buying habits of the audience, and the interiors. Everything looks the same. But there will always be those who want to express their individuality and search for inimitable, unique products.

6

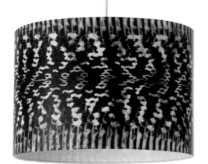

7

Brunklaus   46/47

The Dish from a Designer

THE EVOLUTION AND REVOLUTION OF HOME
PRODUCT DESIGN

Johanna Grawunder

She was making crème brûlée with her husband's
blowtorch. "It works better than the little propane
thing from the gourmet store," she said. Crème
brûlée? Maison brûlée! I mentioned that it seemed
a bit like cutting butter with a chain saw. "Well, no,"
she said, "because if the butter is really so hard,
you just zap it a few seconds in the microwave—
six seconds for Häagen-Dazs."

In today's home, the green tea powder is still
whipped with a little bamboo whisk, and the flatware on
the table should be spotless, as always. Damask is still
the textile of choice for formal dinners and a perfect
omelet can be made in cast iron, Emerilware, or Teflon, it

does not matter. (Americans have large amounts of Teflon
in their blood, by the way.) Some traditions and rules do
not change, some do. For most westerners, home living is
not fundamentally different from what it was years ago.
Most of us still sleep on a bed and use dishes, utensils,
tables, and chairs. Jerry Seinfeld even points out how
incredibly well we sit in chairs, almost as if we were
designed for the purpose: look how our bodies bend in
exactly the right places for the chair? We have some
newer "musts" like Cuisinarts and George Foreman Grills,
but do they really make us cook or eat better?

Many home products have been designed over
centuries by layering information and innovation to the
point of perfection: spoon, fork, teacup, sugar bowl,
bread knife, scissors, water kettle, cheese grater, whisk,
spatula, and the previously mentioned chair. It is not
necessary to revolutionize these designs. What is
interesting is to interpret them using the few variables
we are occasionally given, such as new materials
or techniques, cultural resonance and the "spirit of our
times," or the more influential but even more rare
behavioral modification that sometimes occurs. Design
changes now that we suck coffee through a slit in
a plastic lid while driving as opposed to sitting down to
high tea. The constant cross fertilization of cultures
and rituals, such as the influence of Asian cuisine on
contemporary Western cooking, has changed some
basic elements and materials on our tables. Products for

the home are being constantly redesigned for these reasons with slight modifications, a gentle tweaking of evolutional design.

There is another world, though—a parallel universe of home products where tabula rasa design can occur. In this world, new design solutions stem from new conditions: 24-7 lifestyles, people occupying what were once considered uninhabitable spaces with limited natural light and ventilation, the state of our cities as they fall into an ungraceful middle age, the impersonality of services, the hardness of our environ-ment, and the dictates of a cynical commercial culture intent on marketing the lowest-common-denominator television, government, diet, entertainment, and lifestyle. In this world, there are new problems to be addressed by architecture and design. In this world, products for the home are not really evolving, they are coming into being. They exist contemporaneously with the elderly statesmen of home products: the teapot, the wine glass, the towel rack. But they address problems never encountered before, problems that go beyond conve-nience and economy (a DustBuster deals with those) into existential ideas about the way we live now. I think these new problems—more so than new materials, computer programs, or production technologies—may be the catalysts for the most interesting new design. My design process is the same whether based in the historical context of evolutionary design or the more temporal one of new problems. I design physical, practical, and material spaces and objects referencing the constant (and perhaps eternal) desires, sensations, physicality, and emotions of people.

In a third parallel universe, it does not matter. If you hate your wife, you will hate having tea with her whether you are using a fine antique Chinese ensemble, a contemporary design in stainless steel, or a paper cup. Likewise, if you passionately desire your lover, the floor of the Black Rock Desert is as comfortable as any thousand-thread-count white-duvet-covered king size bed at a five-star hotel. Some things cannot be solved or improved by design. These comprise the real gifts of life, and in the face of these, design is merely terrestrial.

After completing her studies in architecture at California Polytechnic State University in San Luis Obispo in 1985, spend-ing her final year at the university's foreign campus in Florence, Johanna Grawunder joined Sottsass Associati in Milan, a partner there four years later. Grawunder has been behind some of the most prestigious architectural projects of the studio, such as Casa Wolf in Colorado and the Ernest Mourmans House in Belgium. Now based in San Francisco and Milan, she is currently working on her own architectural, interior, and lighting design projects and is a frequent lecturer throughout Europe. Grawunder has held numerous solo exhibitions and collaborated with such companies as Flos, Boffi Salviati, JG Durand, Mikasa, and Christofle of France.

1

3. Between Two Chairs, 2002. Laser-cut metal, water cut foam, steel frame. Produced by Bahnsen.

1. Retreat funnel chair, 1998. Metal thread, angora wool. Produced by One Off.

2. Folda chair, 2000. Steel frame, foam, felt, wool. Produced by Bahnsen.

Louise Campbell
Less Limits

Born:
Copenhagen, Denmark

Practice:
Copenhagen, Denmark

I find being a female designer today very straightforward. My personal issues as a woman are precisely reflected in the need for radical changes in the material world. *I only need to look at my own little day-to-day complications to see exactly what is needed in the market.* I am continually frustrated with the products I find myself forced to use—they just do not appeal to me. My computer is hard to the touch and ugly as sin to look at. I believe I would do better work if my keypad

2

3

was made in a softer material and was better integrated with my work surface; if my monitor could easily be cleaned of coffee and tobacco stains; if my mouse was heated, so that it felt like a friend and not an enemy; if my hard disc made gentler, more motivating sounds. This is the attitude I take to my design of furniture.

I loathe the huge sofas that are priced by the cubic foot (is this a phallic complex that is being satisfied?). They are only elegant on the surface, filled with medium density fiberboard and glue and blue foam and more glue. So I designed the opposite: a lightweight skinny little sofa, no less comfortable, but far more honest in its use of materials and form. I added a touch of flexibility, and choose the finest wool and felt for upholstery. The purchaser deserves something special—and honest.

I hated being embarrassed about the mess my clothes were always creating in the bedroom. So, I designed the Casual Cupboards, which make a positive point out of not ironing, not folding, not sorting.

4

5

6

4. Honesty chair, 1999. Ash wood with duvet. Produced by Jacob Trolle.

5. Casual cupboards, 2000. Ash, sycamore or cherry veneer. Produced by Bahnsen.

6. Bille Goes Zen, 2003. Ash wood. Produced by Lars Bille.

7. Seesaw sofa, 2002. Wood and steel frame, foam and wool upholstery. Produced by Erik Jørgensen Møbelfabrik.

They are shaped in a way that makes the clothes look good no matter how violently you shove them in. Truth be told—are clothes not the most frequently updated autonarrative possessions we have? Why should we hide them away?

And so it goes with all my work. I try to improve the awfully unpleasant visits to waiting rooms by designing furniture, such as the Seesaw sofa, for the mind as well as the body. I regularly design chairs that are not meant for production, but should be seen as ideas about

what furniture can do for you: make you feel safe, make you feel special, cradle you, give you something to fiddle with, give you something to think about. I design lamps that remind you of what light is really all about. You never look at the light source of the sun itself; instead you enjoy the millions of changes it undergoes as it filters through the landscape. This is rarely true when you look at most indoor lighting. I take the shadows of all my pieces as seriously as their physical form. A piece of furniture with a clumsy shadow is bound to be clumsy itself.

7

There is an overflow of two types of products—
the extremely practical, which sacrifices aesthetics
and emotional values for the sake of function, and the
very playful, which puts form and imagery before
function. I seek to make a third type by allowing myself
to be sensitive. I believe in taking the things that
surround me seriously, making small, gentle changes,
and working within emotional points of focus.

1

2

1. Slot screen, 2004. Steel tube, fabric.

2. Two-Way stool, 2001. Powder-coated composite wood.

3. Spiral shelves, 2002. Baltic plywood.

Jennifer Carpenter
Truck Product Architecture

Born:
Honolulu, USA

Practice:
New York, USA

After graduating from Columbia University with my master of architecture in hand, burned out on concepts and theories, I started a handbag company. I wanted to create things with a quick design/build gratification. I had designed a molded-leather bag that I was sure would be a runaway hit because people I did not know constantly commented on the one I carried on my back. I made some samples, paid $2,500 for space at a trade show, and was in business. Or so I thought. I quickly learned that when you have bills to pay, good design is

3

not enough; my good design also had to get to market on time—and it had to sell. I worked around-the-clock for eight weeks filling orders after the show. I prayed for no reorders, and my prayers were answered.

Eager to join a sound practice with high design standards, I went to work at Rogers Marvel Architects in New York and became a licensed architect. While there, I discovered that I loved designing furnishings and fixtures for clients' spaces. I worked closely with fabricators to engineer the details of custom pieces,

making sure they were well built and also affordable. With Rogers Marvel's support, I launched the company Truck Product Architecture soon thereafter. Now I collaborate with design-focused manufacturers and distributors to realize my products, as these companies are better at the business of design than I could ever be. I do not have the kind of control I had over my bags, but I have a much wider reach. It is a welcome tradeoff.

Finding opportunities for collaboration has not been easy. While large European furniture and

4

5

product manufacturers typically solicit—and credit—independent designers, this relationship is much less common in the States. Americans seem to value design more and more, but they are frequently offered a kind of good-design, mass-market surface treatment rather than true rethinking. It is up to designers like me to make our value more apparent both to manufacturers and to consumers.

I am currently collaborating with the venerable tabletop corporation Mikasa, and we are both excited about the prospects of the relationship. Working with a company like Truck is a good, low-risk investment for them: the royalties they pay me mount up only when sales do, and crediting and promoting a designer is good for their business. I benefit from advanced technology, sophisticated distribution, and market know-how that I could not access on my own. In this and other partnerships, *it is our joint goal to send the message that modern design is not an all-or-nothing proposition—*

6. TRUCKids SitStep and FriendBench, 2002. Painted composite wood, Baltic plywood. Produced by Offi.

4. Take It Easy table, 2003. Aluminum tubing, painted wood. Produced by Mikasa/Studio Nova.

5. Tambour table, 2003. Solid wood, Baltic plywood.

6

that a Truck table can live in the same space as an heirloom rug. The market for modern design in the United States is not even close to saturated, and there is plenty of work to be done. When Americans are not buying enough milk the Dairy Council pools its resources to send the message that milk is good for us and makes other things taste better. If only designers could do the same.

1

1. Swing Unit 5 cabinets, 2001–2003. MDF or lacquered surfaces, chrome and silver-coated castors. Produced by Zoltan.

2. Mick table, 2000. Lacquered MDF, polished stainless steel. Produced by Lemongras.

Carmen Cheong
Lemongras

Born:
Singapore City, Singapore

Practice:
Munich, Germany

My partner Moritz Engelbrecht and I have been working together since we met at the Royal College of Art in London. Our collaboration has always been a perfect match between Moritz, the furniture designer, and me, the industrial designer. We founded Lemongras after we moved to Munich, aiming to produce fresh, illustrative and usable products.

As opposed to Moritz, who gets most of his ideas through materials and components, *I tend to translate images into products.*

2

For example, a bowling pin is literally transformed into a
peppermill or a new lamp is formed by collaging or
filtering several objects such as a dress and a basket.
I call this method of merging different objects together
to create a new product "image/object translation."

Due to our different cultural backgrounds, what
interests us most is combining our influences to
create a more international language. This brings our
products a greater dimensionality. We regard designers
as individuals who give an object an individualistic

character. This perspective provides an appreciable
difference from a mainstream product made for global
use. How people in the future see their homes will
depend on how individual or how mainstream they think.

3

4

3. Nutopener, 2001. Polished stainless steel. Produced by Lemongras.

4. Looper wall lamp, 2001.
Polycarbonate, color foils, white
cable. Produced by Lemongras.

5. Pin pepper, salt, and spice
grinders, 1998. Maplewood, ceramic.
Produced by Lemongras.

6. Bowl, 2001. Wood, nylon.
Produced by Lemongras.

5

6

1

1. Girl's Best Friend conceptual rock/weapon and lipstick mirror, 2002. Stainless steel with one flat mirror-polished face.

2. Kirilume light, 2001. Electroluminescent film.

Jessica Corr

Born:
Baltimore, USA

Practice:
New York, USA

When I entered college, I did not have an exact plan. I just knew I wanted to make things. It was a pretty basic desire. I was initially drawn to glassblowing, where I found the creative process to have an equal physical and spiritual intensity. There was also the immediate gratification of crafting a beautiful object that I found so alluring. At the same time, and for similar reasons, I began to work in furniture and product design. The scale and immediacy of the work appealed to me, as did the equal parts of physical and intellectual labor

2

required to produce it. What ultimately pushed me toward furniture and product design was the satisfaction and inspiration I receive when a clear interaction exists between people and the work itself. If I had not become a designer, my curiosity in what is universally pleasing to people and why would have led me to become an anthropologist.

Products must be layered, like personalities. They function for us on many levels, both interactive (physical) and reactive (emotional). While its pragmatic aspects must not fail, a successful product elicits a rich and varied intuitive response to social perceptions and the nature of materials.

Over the years, I have invested a significant amount of time researching materials and manufacturing processes. I have also used the very concept of mass production as an impetus for creating work. And although I may bring the work to fruition using self-produced prototypes or small production runs, I design each piece with mass-production in mind.

3

4

5

Concept, function, and the methodologies of fabrication
are all equal contributors to my work. Each has a
significant presence for me. This balance often blurs my
perception of what is considered art, craft, or design.
Furthermore, by uniting two disparate concepts,
materials, or forms, I am able to integrate the elements
of surprise and contrast that are so fundamental to
my work.

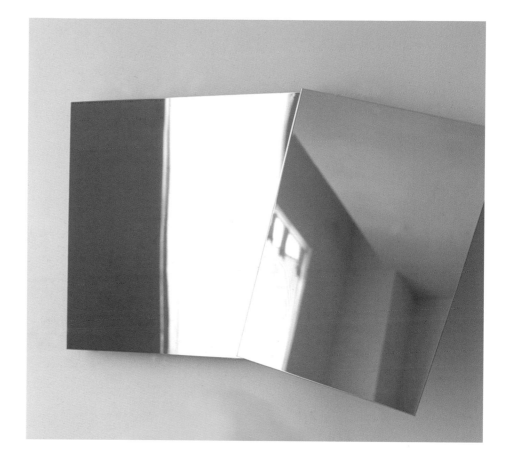

5. Eternal wood tiles, 2002. Wood veneer strips suspended in ultra-violet-protected rubber.

6. Fiancé mirror, 2002. Mirror-polished stainless steel.

3. Sir Donkey John Doe pillows, 2002. Soft, self-skinning, slow-recovery foam, gold leaf.

4. Eternal carpet, 2001. Carpet suspended in ultraviolet-protected rubber. Designed by Collaborative.

1

1. Téo from 2 to 3 Siesta stool, 1999. Wood structure, high-resilience foam, double tufted felt. Produced by Domeau & Pérès.

2. License to Build sofa and children's game, 2000. High-resilience foam, cotton fabric. Produced by Domeau & Pérès.

Matali Crasset
Matali Crasset Productions

Born:
Châlons-en-Champagne, France

Practice:
Paris, France

My parents are farmers and I grew up in a small village of fifty people. Design was very far from me and my culture. I discovered design by chance at the university in a marketing class; it was a revelation in my life. From that moment I decided to be a designer.

I work with a diverse group of clients in very different areas. I try to be flexible, but I also want to instill my own methodology. Product development is a complex process, and to guarantee the quality of the product you really need to control it. More importantly,

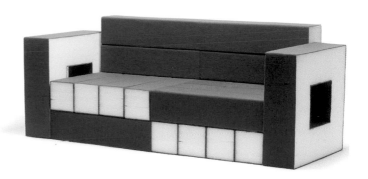

2

you need to make the concept progress in a creative way. You have to find a means to make your object accessible. It could be a very specific and experimental project with self-production or a more evolved object with a large company. Communication is part of the work. It belongs to the definition of a product. The more you communicate, the more people will understand your approach and ask you to collaborate with them.

Many of the challenges and obstacles to good design come from the big-company landscape.

Companies are changing dramatically, which is affecting their ability to make good decisions. *Creativity is fragile. We need a certain stability and the potential to work in a long-term process to really do our jobs properly.*

I do not believe in a design revolution, but I do believe objects can help evolve our behavior to be more in accordance with what we need today—more hospitable and generous. In the future, products

3

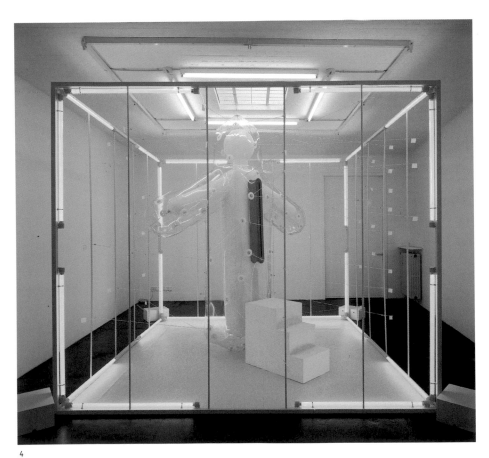

4

3. Pouf 1, Pouf 4, and Pouf 6, 2003. High-density foam, polyurethane coating.

4. Update Three Spaces in One: Energizer conceptual light bath-room, 2002. Bathroom fixtures, plastic, fluorescent tube lighting. Curated by Andrea Hoyer and Mike Meiré. Produced by Dornbracht Bathvisions.

5. Update Three Spaces in One: Phytolab conceptual chlorophyll bathroom, 2002. Bathroom fixtures, plastic, potted plants. Curated by Andrea Hoyer and Mike Meiré. Produced by Dornbracht Bathvisions.

will be more malleable, giving us the liberty to do things without blocking us in with defined sociological atti-tudes. These societal changes and emerging behaviors are the inspiration for my work.

5

6. Table tray and shelves, 2003.
Metal structure, wood and metal
trays. Produced by Top-Mouton.

7. Happy Bar, HI Hotel, Nice,
France, 2003. Interior, furniture,
and dishware.

8. Soundstation radio/alarm clock,
1996/1998. ABS plastic, soft
electronic card. Artistic direction
by Philippe Starck. Produced by
Lexon with Thomson Mult·media.

7

1

2

Sophie Demenge
R+D Design and Oeuf

Born:
Paris, France

Practice:
New York, USA

I have always wanted to be an industrial designer, without knowing it. I knew one could be an artist or an architect, but was not aware of anything in between. I heard the term "industrial design" for the first time in San Francisco when I was about twenty-three. I was intrigued by it, took a class at the city college, and loved it. So I researched and applied to design schools, and off I went to New York.

Halfway through my education at Pratt Institute, I met a nice boy, a self-taught designer, who is now my

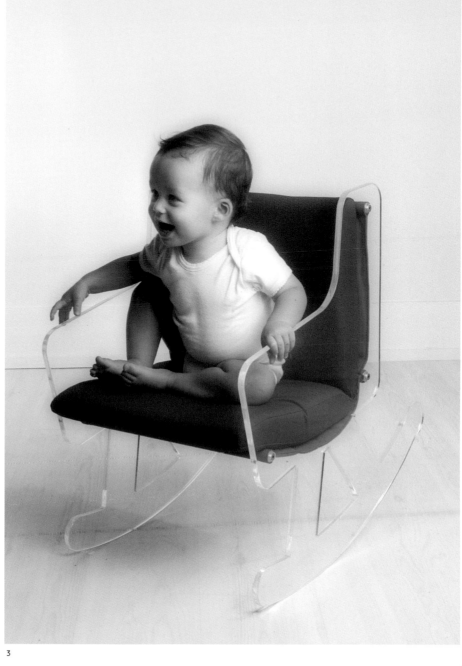

3

1. Osi leather table, 1999. Steel, leather.

2. Sugar cups, 2000. Ceramic.

3. Baby lounger, 2C03. Acrylic, upholstery.

husband and father of Mae. We blindly and enthusiastically decided to start a business together right after I graduated. Here we are, four wonderful, frustrating, joyful, painful years later, miraculously still in business, still quite optimistic, and feeling very lucky we do what we do.

I see design as a vehicle to express myself. I tend to favor the intimate and playful. My inspiration comes from everywhere and nowhere, whether it is walking down the street, finding an interesting piece of hardware and imagining what should be around it, making furniture with my daughter from clementine peels, watching people in the subway, going to the Met, or soaking in the tub with a notebook nearby—just living, really. *When inspiration happens, it fills me with enormous energy and joy, and feels like it is never going to stop.* It brings this great rush, which reminds me why I love it so much and why I put up with all the business stuff. And with no resistance at all,

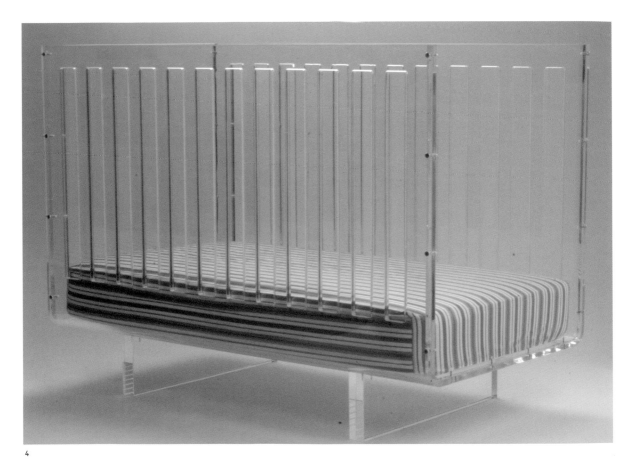

4

I indulge once again in the adventure of the creative process. The biggest challenge is to bring this embryo of an idea to fruition and, for me, that is when "being an adult" kicks in.

Every project is different. The overall process is the same (excitement, frustration, doubt, technicalities, making the damn thing, letting it be for a while, back and forth, lots of coffee, and excitement again), but each design has a different way of revealing itself as a completed piece. I am continually surprised by the result.

It is as though at the end it is not mine anymore but rather has become its own self—with a life, a personality of its own, independent of pure functionality. This is a good thing, as it enables a relationship.

The disadvantages of self-production and owning your own business are that you have to do it all, all the time: make decisions constantly, struggle with price versus volume, etc. You must have an understanding of every single aspect of your business, and accept that designing takes around five percent of your time and

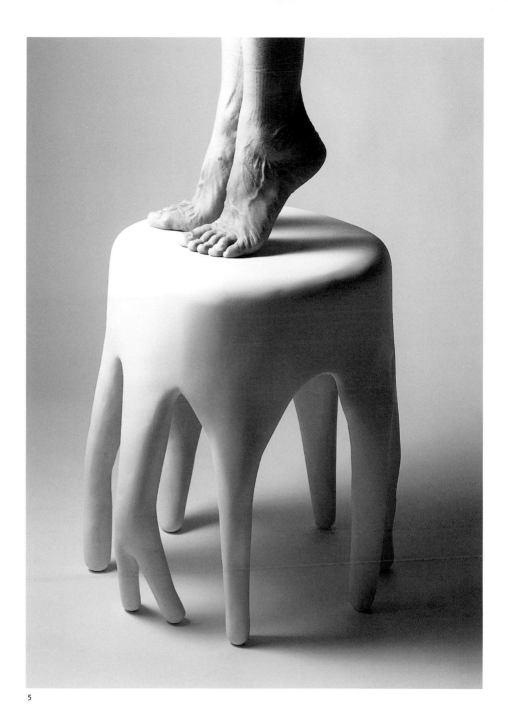

5

running a business and keeping it alive takes the other ninety-five percent. The advantages are that it is all yours and, yes, you can go to Fire Island on a Tuesday. Self-production never allows you to become complacent; there is nowhere to hide.

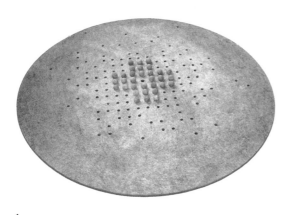

1

2

Florence Doléac

Born:
Toulouse, France

Practice:
Paris, France

1. Tapis de Société, Solitaire game board/carpet, 2001. Natural felt. Produced by Galerie Aline Vidal.

2. Biscuit Cover edible coffee cover, 2003. Flour, butter, egg, sugar, almond powder.

3. Robot fruit and vegetable holder, 2001. Ceramic. Designed by Florence Doléac/RADI Designers. Produced by Andreas Bergmann and Claude Aïello, Vallau-is.

I graduated from L'Ecole Nationale Supérieure de Création Industrielle—ENSCI/Les Ateliers in Paris in 1994, where I met my future RADI Designers colleagues. Laurent Massaloux, Robert Stadler, Olivier Sidet, and I had begun our collaboration as students and, in 1997, cofounded the company. It was the beginning of an intense and fruitful collaboration. In 2003 I decided to strike out on my own. While teaching at the Ecole Cantonnale d'Art de Lausanne, I produced projects and exhibited work in art

3

galleries. Galerie Aline Vidal in Paris has represented me since 2002.

My work is focused on the poetic, the conceptual, and the improbable. My considerations are not of an industrial nature but rather a dialogue between design and art, in which the means of presentation and production oscillate. This constitutes my distinctive and unique position in the contemporary design world. I not only play on the tension between production and exhibition, providing incongruous solutions, but also examine the very concepts of functionality and uselessness.

Being an industrial designer and a woman is still relatively rare and therefore exciting, as all unbeaten paths are wont to be. Operating within a masculine and technical milieu, which is in fact often impractical, is bound to be productive. Perhaps I became a designer because I grew up in a creative environment that was a constant source of stimulation. So I do not see it as a job, but like breathing—my way of being and

4. La chaise mise à nu, 2002. Wool felt. Produced by Galerie Aline Vidal.

thinking. Letting my thoughts wander, confounding the useful and the useless, obsessively observing people— these are my defining postures. Everything comes from this. *For me, life is nothing but a grand theatrical show, and I take pleasure in being attuned to it.*

From this perspective, self-production enables me to create with more meaning, even though the production is itself limited. Of course, mass production is exciting because the stakes are high, but too narrow

a mandate can spoil all the fun of a project. One must remain vigilant. I like to practice both mass and self-production, so long as I am free to think and the project remains respectable. I cannot design an object to whose use or consumption I object.

On this point, I hope that industrial design will evolve toward less materialistic and coded practices than today's, and that objects and their functions will be less authoritarian; we have become enslaved to them. The house could be a place for personal imagination. It

constitutes one of the few places where one can
explore one's fantasies. But the image of the ideal
house is overly determined by social representations
and codes rather than by its ability to conform to
one's own idiosyncrasies. This is what I suggest in my
work; I offer hypotheses, alternatives to these absurd
and excessive constraints.

5

6

7

5. Poignèe molle door handle, 2002.
Balloon, flour, metal, wood.

6. Télélumine light, 2002.
Television, painted wood table,
brass structure, Lycra. Produced by
Galerie Aline Vidal.

7. Trou de mémoire calendar, 2003.
Clothes pins, double-sided tape.
Produced by Galerie Aline Vidal.

8. Passages, 2002. Wooden doors,
paint. Produced by Galerie Aline
Vidal.

1

The Dish from an Art Director

ADAPTING PRODUCTION TO THE OBJECT

Patrizia Moroso

In the Babel-like confusion of contemporary life, the languages of design are legion. Everything and its opposite really do seem to work. I get the impression that today's trend-setting products have been created by the slogans of communications wizards, not by real needs or changing tastes. They are dreamed up by committees of advertising executives, who then craft sophisticated means to sell them. "Belonging strategies," as ad people call them, involve creating imaginary realities where everything, from clothing to cars, is carefully calculated. They communicate a desire to own this or that object so that the consumer can feel part of a group. The metamessages they subliminally transmit in commercials and posters say,

"Do as you like, but watch out! If you don't buy this, you are out. You don't matter."

I am horror-struck at this world split into tribes. I perceive it as a genuine imposition. In this context, anything is valid and acceptable, provided it gets made and launched and fits into a group. In order to stand out, industrial design has to amaze by continually offering new features. The sheer quantity of objects manufactured becomes insane, while their quality and creativity suffer.

All this frenzy simply does not interest me. As the art director for Moroso, a high-end Italian furniture manufacturer, I have never consulted a marketing expert to find out what the next big thing will be or which way the market will go. If you follow the advertising, you are drawn into an empty, ephemeral world that belongs to the moment, not to time. It is a world that leaves me indifferent. I prefer to explore other avenues.

My work springs from a desire to create products with soul, which is the antithesis of making worlds in which to belong. I strive to stay absolutely faithful to project values before I think about sales strategies, which should be a logical consequence, not a point of departure. I am aware that Moroso demands a commitment from users: they have to choose the particular product most suitable for them. This is the exact opposite of the buying behavior induced in a world where everything is prepackaged.

Instead of worrying about what the next fashion is going to be, I think we should be asking ourselves what design is. Achille Castiglioni used to say that design means inventing something that doesn't exist to perform a function better. Design is research and planning, things that companies should embrace today as never before. Each project is one designer's personal response to a specific problem, so there will be many possible solutions to any given issue. The solutions may be more or less radical, and more or less widely accepted, but they will always be consistent with the designer's specific worldview and culture. My job is simply deciding with whom to work. I leave to the designer the task of investigating—with his or her own individual taste and intelligence—a product type or the solution to a problem.

I believe it is important to work with the designer using both production- and non-production-related reasoning. The mind explores better when it moves in complete freedom. Nor should we underestimate the extent to which aesthetics is a vehicle for innovation. I was particularly interested in this a few years ago, at the turn of the millennium, when the feeling of a fast-approaching newness was strong and tangible.

The new millennium arrived just before Moroso's fiftieth anniversary. What better way for a design-driven company to celebrate than by inviting fifty designers to have their say? From the start, I wanted the resulting exhibition, Off Scale, to be exploratory, to emphasize the value of the idea with respect to the product. Giving shape to these ideas was not easy. In quite a few cases, the effort of adapting production to the object, instead of the object to production, gave us the stimulus to try out new technologies and materials that later became the foundation for a product's success.

The marvelous Off Scale experience generated many new products and much vitality. It created a determination to make even more connections between experiences, people, habits, sectors, and consumers. It also brought me to understand that observing different creative realities—specifically, that of the art world—is a good point of departure for design experimentation. There is an affinity between Moroso and contemporary art. It derives from the conviction that space is the sum of the relationships that every object—whether it is unique or mass-manufactured—establishes within itself. The relationships change depending on whether their magical power of surprise, or their function of use, predominates. It is on this borderline that art and design interact.

Personally, I do not believe that an object can have a gendered aesthetic. But I do believe in the feminine qualities of products. I think our products have them, thanks to their sensuous lines, their interplay of mass and void, their invitation to physical contact, and their attention to covering materials. I think the difference between the work of female and male designers lies in

the ways they operate. The feminine way of thinking
is rarely linear or direct. It is a thinking that goes ahead,
then turns back, and is always open to a possible
change of direction.

I find working with a woman more intimate, and
more enjoyable, than working with a man. It is like chatting
with a friend or sharing an insight. It means doing things
not because you have to, but from the heart, from friend-
ship, from a sense of fun. I have never been dogmatic
in my thinking. Rigidity annoys me. Usually, this approach
is seen as unprofessional, but working for pleasure, passion, and love is very productive. I can say that for me
as a woman, working with a woman is the best experience
I can have. It is a pity that it is such a rare one.

1. Bloomy chair, 2004. Flexible steel frame, flame-retardant injected
cold foam, wool upholstery, zipper. Designed by Patricia Urquiola.
Produced by Moroso. Photo by Alessandro Paderni.

*Patrizia Moroso is art director of Moroso SpA, a high-end con-
temporary furniture manufacturer founded in 1952 by Agostino
Moroso in Italy. After growing up over the factory, she took up her
studies at the DAMS (Department of Art, Music and the
Performing Arts) at the University of Bologna. After graduating,
she joined the family company and has since managed to
change it in many ways. Moroso SpA has earned a reputation for
its commitment to innovation in technology and design, and its
insistence on craft-quality manufacturing standards.*

1

1. Sweater lamp, 2003. Wool yarn, acrylic, electrical parts.

2. Puzzle screen, 2000. Powder-coated steel.

Rie Egawa

egawa + zbryk

Born:
Kobe, Japan

Practice:
Kansas City, USA

Since when I was very young, I have always loved drawing and making things, so it is only natural that I became an artist and designer. I never wanted to be anything else. Although I still enjoy drawing and painting, I am currently more drawn to three-dimensional work, such as sculpture and product design. *It is the creation and appreciation of art that makes us truly human and we should bring more art into our everyday lives.* I worked as a textile

2

designer for the fashion industry in New York for many years before I met my partner and husband, Burgess Zbryk. We started collaborating as Egawa + Zbryk, creating a wide range of home furnishing designs and art.

My inspirations are everywhere—everything that stimulates my senses, more often visual and tactile senses, such as light, color, shape, and texture, both natural and man-made, both micro and macro. I am fascinated by science and technology. Organic forms or seemingly-random-yet-orderly patterns found in nature often influence my designs.

I enjoy being hands-on, and most of our prototypes are made in house. Self-production means that the designer's creative and original idea and intention stay undiluted and therefore pure. Of course it is the ultimate fun to be able to produce whatever I desire without any negotiation by committee, but at the same time this way of working is extremely time consuming and cost prohibitive.

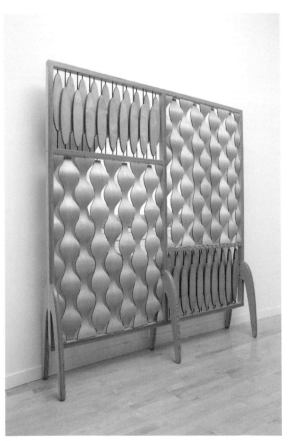

3

4

It would be ideal to collaborate with companies or manufacturers that can afford cutting-edge technological innovations to create exciting and compelling products, all while striving to be conscientious of our environment and of basic human needs and comforts. Seeking out manufacturers who truly understand and appreciate good design is not only difficult but highly competitive. There is no shortage of poorly or over-designed products out in the market.

What makes my design team, Egawa + Zbryk, unique and interesting is that even though both partners have very similar tastes, we each bring a very different flavor and view, whether it is gender or culture, into the creative process. We enjoy sketching and brainstorming together and often one finishes what the other starts. I think I tend to bring more emotion and spontaneity to the table, and Burgess brings an engineering and detail-oriented view. But we both look for simple construction, clean forms, and that element that gives a

3. Oggi screen, 1993. Birch plywood, steel.

4. String chair, 2000. Hoop pine,
birch veneer, polyester cord,
stainless steel.

5. Pod lamp, 1998. Birch plywood,
Plexiglas, electrical parts.

5

distinct personality to everything we create. I would love
to keep working as a hybrid between designer and
artist, creating both mass-produced designs and one-of-
a-kind art, always staying fluid, diverse, and, above all,
passionate.

1

1. H seat, 2001. Steel, wool cushion.

2. High single seat, 2001. Steel.

3. Love bench, 2001. Lacquered wood, wool cushion.

Han Teng

Han Teng New York

Born:
Nanjin, China

Practice:
New York, USA

I grew up in China during the Cultural Revolution. My imagination, like that of many children, served as entertainment as well as a means for survival. *The simple and profound beauty inherent in my surroundings has always stirred my creativity. As a child, stones became mountains and fish became chariots.* My mother recognized my creative passion early and encouraged me in my study of art and graphic design.

2

3

When I first came to New York, I worked and quickly became interested in clothing design as a salesperson at Bloomingdale's. Eventually I developed pleated scarves, which I wore and sold right out of my shoulder bag. The scarves became very popular and led me to open a development studio in the Garment District. But my appetite for design knows no bounds: I run the gamut from fashion to furniture.

My design work is simple and architectural. I love using color and mixing materials to create texture.

There is a "bridge" theme in my work, reflecting a fusion of my life in China and my subsequent decades in America. I think my work imparts fun, lightheartedness, and a graphic awareness. Self-production affords me the freedom to explore many different dimensions in the design process and to produce something uniquely touched by the designer. Mass production reaches many people but in a less personal way. My vision is to produce objects that add thoughtful beauty and joy to people's everyday lives. Finding a manufacturer

4

5

who understands and appreciates this vision, and wants to work toward translating it to a large-scale market, is difficult for obvious reasons.

     Today most of my friends treasure their antique possessions above all else. This is so in part because a lot of contemporary design lacks the workmanship that was once inherent in even the most utilitarian pieces. I strive to infuse design with warmth and unexpected detail. My origin as a graphic designer combined with my joyful intentions are also reflected in my work. As an

artist I think of myself purely in terms of being a person without consideration of gender—endeavoring to touch another human spirit through my work.

4. Melon bowl, 2003. Clay.

5. Pleated plate, 2002. Ceramic.

6. Black dress, 1994. Poly organza/
poly georgette.

1

Monica Förster

Born:
Stockholm, Sweden

Practice:
Stockholm, Sweden

After making many strange projects in school, I was convinced that no one would hire me, and so I decided to start my own business. That meant a learning curve in which I discovered, among many things, how to make the right decisions at the right time.

In order for my designs to be as widely available as possible, I work only in collaboration with producers. This relationship allows me to make use of both the advanced techniques and technologies and

1. Tray table, 2003. Lacquered wood, polyurethane, chrome. Produced by Offecct.

2. Nola Sun and Cake tables, 2004. Indoor/outdoor laser-cut steel. Produced by Nola Industrier AB.

2

the professional experience a manufacturer offers. Working with an accomplished, expert team is a big part of the fun in being a designer. Together, it is possible to do better work.

Design is becoming more flexible and adaptable, yet I believe it is hard to avoid past influences. Male designer or female designer—does it really matter? Isn't it really about making the best projects possible and having manufacturers who believe in them? And isn't it also about creating a network of men and women who are good at what they do and fun to work with?

3

4

3. Load cordless portable lamp, 2001. Rotation-molded polyethylene, rechargeable battery, low-energy bulb. Produced by David Design.

4. Silikon lamp, 1999. Molded, flexible silicone, low-energy bulb, electrical parts. Produced by David Design.

5. Cloud portable inflatable room, 2002. Ripstop nylon, sound-decreasing textile bag with fan. Produced by Offecct.

5

6

6. Mix round vase, 2003. Crystal, Plexiglas. Produced by Skurf.

7. Mix round bowl, 2003. Crystal, Plexiglas. Produced by Skurf.

8. Mix Konisk bowl, 2003. Crystal, Plexiglas. Produced by Skurf.

9. Moon Cactus carpet, 2003. Short- and long-cut wool. Produced by E&Y.

10. Glow in the Dark toilet seat, 1995. Injection-molded plastic with photo-luminescent plastic. Produced by Magis.

7

8

9

10

Förster   98/99

1

1. Bombay vases, 2002. Glass.
Produced by Skruf.

2. Not shelves, 1993. Plexiglas.

3. Messiah shelves, 1993.
Plexiglas.

Anki Gneib

I like to find forms that already exist and am inspired by ordinary shapes that can be transferred to new materials and functions. The design process is a fascinating journey, leading to a result that is not known from the start. I like to integrate playfulness in both the process and its resolution.

Environments and lifestyles that are different, odd, or foreign to me have influenced my designs.

The Messiah and Not shelves were among my first

Born:
London, UK

Practice:
Stockholm, Sweden

2

3

professional work and define it well. They were inspired by Persian calligraphy, a highly stylized print used in the beautiful mosaics of Persian mosques. The words "messiah" and "not," extracted from the Koran, emerge in the form of shelves.

Design is a means of communication and of developing relationships. In working with producers, I initially refer to myself and my own needs. But ultimately the process is very much a team effort in identifying solutions and discovering new directions and different ways of manufacturing. I find inspiration in the company's history, frame work, and most importantly, their vision. New manufacturing technology and materials, as well as new design and creativity, reflect the world we live in, socially, economically and environmentally.

The industrial world is dominated by men and male values. However, women have a lot to say. We are half the population of the world and the current majority in design schools. But everyone is an individual, with an individualistic way of

4

communicating and expressing oneself.

    In the future, there will be more collective think-
ing in design. In some ways, this could strengthen
personal expression and ultimately result in a broader
and more varied range of creativity, both emotionally
and geographically.

4. Hambo chest of drawers, 1998.
Lacquered wood.

5. L.A.P.D. carpet, 2001.
Fingerprint pattern in wool.
Produced by Adesso.

6. Kennedy table and stool, 2001.

Molded fiberglass table, wood
frame, nonflammable foam stuffing,
removable fabric cover stool.
Produced by Offecct.

5

6

1

Lyn Godley

Born:
Oberlin, USA

Practice:
Blandon, USA

I did not decide to be a designer. I had studied art and had always made things. The decision was more one of making functional things that might sell, in order to support the artwork that did not. Over a period of time, my art and design merged and I quit thinking of the work as two separate entities. When I first started making things it was called "sculpture," then "functional art." Today the same work would be called "design."

When doing one-of-a-kind projects I love being in the studio, up to my elbows in the making of pieces. I also

2

enjoy the cognitive process of designing for production. The decision to work in-house versus designing for larger production really depends on the client, market, distribution, or price-point requirements. I am best suited for the creative part of design, figuring out how it works, then trying it out in a different material, form, or language. I no longer prefer to do volume production in-house. After having done it for fifteen years—for literally hundreds of items, some being made years on end—I still have dreams of drowning in a sea of my Crinkle lamps and coasters.

My work has never defined me. It represents my interests and philosophies, and an inherently tactile relationship to a particular problem. It is a form of communication. It is an outlet. But it is not my only interest, my only means of communicating, or my only outlet. Being a woman, in particular a mother and a teacher, has forced me to balance a life that encompasses a far broader geographic area than solely the territory of designing.

Having children and any career at all is a very difficult balance. I am able to do some of

3

4

my work at home, so I am usually there when my kids get home from school. This is important to me, but it makes for a very short work day and always leads to the feeling that I am not getting enough done, either as a parent or as a designer. It is the greatest challenge I face, this struggle with never having enough time to do all that I want to do. And instead of taking a sensible approach to this dilemma, I continue to take on more as I find interest in so many areas.

On the other hand, I believe this balancing of life has forced me to be a much more compassionate, well-rounded human being. It forces me to think beyond myself, which in the end makes me a better designer. *It would be so easy as a creative person to lock myself in my studio and never come out. Having children has forced me to take part in the world, and not just the world of design.*

3. Crinkle lamp, 1996. Sculpted vinyl, steel, candelabra socket. Designed with Lloyd Schwan for Godley-Schwan.

4. Cut vinyl table lamps, 1994. Vinyl, steel wire, candelabra sockets. Designed with Lloyd Schwan for Godley-Schwan.

5. Elizabeth's Chandelier, 2003. Glass, digital prints, crystal, steel wire, wood, candelabra sockets, compact mini-fluorescent bulbs.

1

Elisabetta Gonzo
(formerly of EG+AV)

Born:
Ravenna, Italy

Practice:
Milan, Italy

Every project starts with material. Material is the foundation of my physical reality, occupying space and assuming shape. By giving material form and function, I add further significance while stimulating the senses of sight and touch. For me, material is more than the fabric of a design, but an end in itself—an object that is the result of an aesthetic dialogue.

If designing were a science, we could compare it to heuristics, a problem-solving technique in which solutions are developed in successive stages, each

2

working from the last. The project becomes one of renunciation: among a number of possibilities, a choice is made.

Design is also a form of poetry. In the same way that the poet does not invent new words but connects existing words in a creative way, the design uses known elements to address the world of shape, form, and function. As designers, we combine these elements to produce unknown but recognizable forms, creating a new language. And *if design is a language,* *then an object must speak to the moment in time in which it exists.* It must also relate to the memory of past associations that make its recognition possible. This delicate alchemy of emergence and permanence makes the object understandable.

The purpose of design is linked first and foremost to action, use, and function. Objects induce us to behave in a certain way. They condition us, educate us, and allow us to live in places in which poetry

3

is not simply ornament, but the very act of creation.
The Greeks had a word, *poiesis,* for this approach.
When undertaking a project, I consider common types
of behavior, usage, relationships, and daily rituals.
Objects help us to perform our routine activities and to
inhabit the present moment in our own home or sphere,
while also connecting with outside worlds. I like to
imagine simple tools, full of history and references, that
are part of everyday life; these are objects that ultimately
access the depths of our souls. Rosemary's cradle, for

example, tells the tale of a fundamental act of life, a
narration based on tradition and memory that could well
have existed for all time.

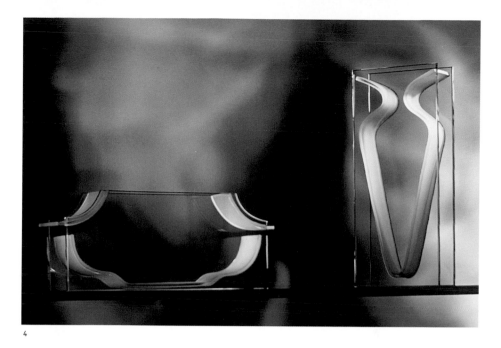

4

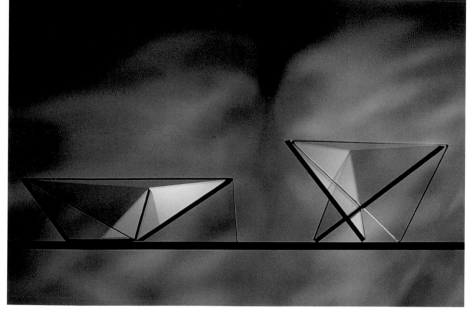

5

3. Rosemary's cradle, 1993. Beech wood, rattan. Designed by EG+AV. Produced by Galleria Luisa delle Piane.

4. Dilettevole and Utile vases, 1992. Glass. Designed by EG+AV. Produced by R.S.V.P.

5. Triangoli and Trapezi center-pieces, 1992. Glass. Designed by EG+AV. Produced by RSVP.

1

Johanna Grawunder

Born:
San Diego, USA

Practice:
Milan, Italy and San Francisco, USA

I am an architect and designer based in Milan, Italy and San Francisco, California. I began working for Ettore Sottsass in 1985 and later became a partner. At Sottsass Associati I collaborated almost exclusively on architecture, interior architecture, and exhibition design. At the same time, I moonlighted with a handful of collaborators to produce limited-edition furniture and lighting collections for several galleries in Europe, as well as products for companies including Boffi Salviati, WMF, JG Durand, Mikasa, and Flos.

2

1. Tritanaopia and Protanaopia lights, 2002. Stainless steel, colored florescent lights, gold mesh. Produced by Gallery Mourmans.

2. X cigar tray, 1999. Black porcelain. Produced by Alfi 21.

3. Jazz vase and bowl, 2002. Digitally cut crystal. Produced by Mikasa.

3

In 2001 I opened my own full-time studio in Milan and San Francisco, collaborating on products for European and U.S. companies, working with a few galleries in Europe, New York, and San Francisco, and doing an occasional architecture or interior architecture project. *In the so-called new world given to us by the information revolution, one can live and work from anywhere. But actually place, like size, matters.* Being based in San Francisco (the capital of technology) and Milan (the capital of design) makes for an interesting and fertile dichotomy. In San Francisco the days are quick and concentrated and involve a lot of email and scanning. The phone often rings at four or five in the morning, which means Italians who can't subtract nine are calling. Milan days are hectic with working and networking but the nights are sometimes filled with pastel drawings or watercolors.

The infrastructure of both studios is flexible and streamlined, with a minimum amount of

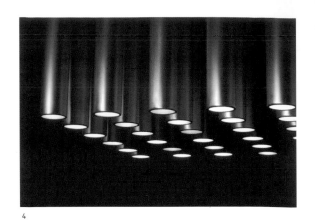

4

5

rhetorical technology. Getting by with a few iBooks and related equipment (and some heavier, strategically placed off-site support) we concentrate on selling ideas, not computer-generated drawings. And so the studios sport an abundance of sensorial information in the form of books, art, music, colored lights (both studios are also used as showrooms for the lights), and "stuff." We do not live in a homogenous, whitewashed world. Why must we work in one?

Generally, my work is informed by how we live now—meaning I work on new solutions to new problems. I have an interest in technology for what it can give us in an iconographic, material, or sensorial way. I also try to work with the raw presence of objects in architecturally scaled designs (like a lot of my lighting fixtures), as well as in actual architecture and interiors, often transposing industrially magnificent elements and materials—such as exposed heavy-duty hinges, industrial work furniture, and bare light

4. 375 hanging light, 2003. Satin-finish aluminum tubes, adjustable steel cables, halogen light system. Produced by Design Gallery Milano.

5. Puddle light table and La Verne wall light, 2003. Puddle: polished aluminum, colored Perspex, adjus-table steel suspension cables, fluorescent tubes. La Verne: steel, painted aluminum, remote-controlled lighting system. Produced by Design Gallery Milano.

6. Indio wall mirror, 2003. Polished aluminum structure, sand-blasted glass, florescent tubes. Produced by Design Gallery Milano.

6

bulbs—into unusual and surprising situations. Other times I like to emphasize through the absence of light or color or the "underdog" properties of a specific place. Then I mix it all up: paint as light, light as furniture, pathways as architecture, transparency as division, thickness as form, color as quality, texture as tempera-ture, and so on. I think a saturated design philosophy is perhaps the most flexible one. It is certainly the most actual and realistic.

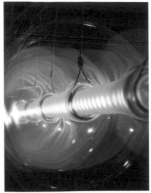

7

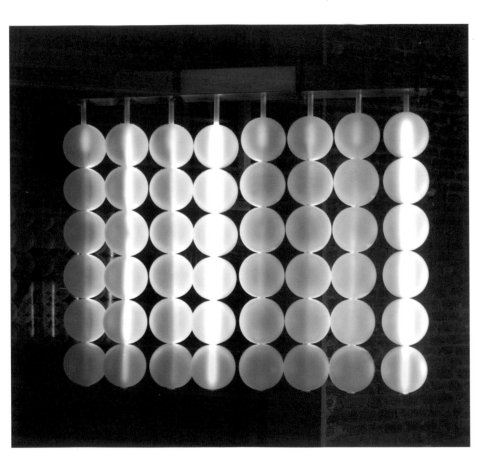

8

Commissioned by Museo di Arte Contemporareo, Siracusa, Sicily and Gallery Roberto Giustini.

10. Stylin' Viper coffee table, 2001. Rubber-painted wood, fluorescent tube lights. Produced for Gallery Post Design.

7. BB hanging light, 2003. Adjustable steel cables, hand-blown sanded glass, integrated circuit of continuous LEDs. Produced by Design Gallery Milano.

8. Ocotillo hanging light, 2003. Polished aluminum, adjustable steel cables, hand-blown sanded glass, integrated circuit of continuous LEDs. Produced by Design Gallery Milano.

9. Wall Lights, permanent outdoor lighting installation, 2003. Fluorescent paint, black light.

9

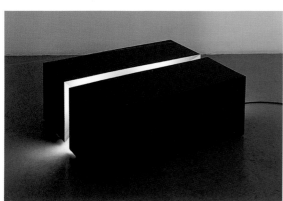

10

1. Tazza Danzante, 2000. Ceramic. Produced by Paola C.

2. Sake bottles, 2003. Ceramic.

3. Section bowls, 2001. Mouth-blown crystal, blown into a mold.

1

Camilla Groth

Born:
Stockholm, Sweden

Practice:
London, UK and Helsinki, Finland

My passion for creating forms began by throwing clay upon a potter's wheel. As time progressed, I began to focus more upon how a specific object affects its user, how it changes the atmosphere of a situation and perhaps even one's own behavior. I love the process of creating a unique piece or finding a shape for a design, but, once I complete a prototype, its reproduction becomes uninteresting to me. This is one of the reasons I consider the possibility of efficient factory reproduction

2

3

while designing the form. Reproduction, however, only applies to pure shapes and does not hold the same value and inspiration that handmade individual pieces do. Therefore my creative process sometimes begins with making a unique piece that then provides inspiration for the next project or reproduced object.

In my work I aim to go a step beyond function, drawing inspiration from the subtle and often-overlooked interactions we have with everyday objects. I try to balance aesthetics with functionality and develop design

concepts that are inspired by various cultures and changes in lifestyle. Although my Scandinavian roots are clearly present in my work, it has also been influenced by my time spent in Japan, Holland, and England. I find design most inspiring when cross-cultural influences result in new solutions and ideas.

4

4. Camouflage cups, 2001. Ceramic.

5. Pleasure eating, 2001. Ceramic.

6. Section vases, 2001. Mouth-blown crystal, blown into a mold.

7. Lens bowl, 1999. Glass. Produced by Iittala.

5

6

7

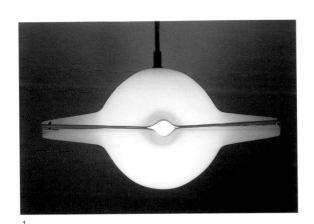

1

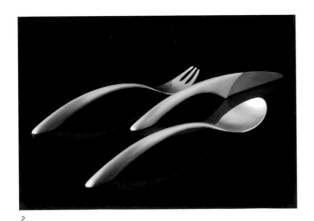

2

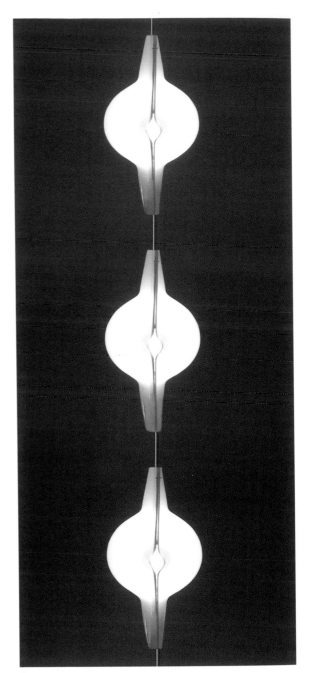

3

Dögg Gudmundsdottir

Dögg Design

Born:
Reykjavik, Iceland

Practice:
Copenhagen, Denmark

I am an Icelandic industrial designer, educated in Italy and Denmark. I am extremely proud of my heritage, as I come from a beautiful country that is full of artistic inspirations. As long as I can remember, I have been interested in art and design. Much of my work comes from ideas derived from the Icelandic natural environment. There you find contrasts and extremes—both raw lava fields and green expanses of trees. Much of this imbues who I am as an artist and inspires my design.

4

Recently I have become more prone to a surrealistic world of forms, manipulating geometric or organic elements that can be combined in countless ways. For example, I used basic square and round shapes to compose unique pieces such as the Túpa, Kite, and Púsl lamps and the ZigZag furniture.

My work is both self-produced and manufactured, and both processes have their pros and cons. Freedom is not having to choose one way or the other—I prefer that the underlying concept of each design dictates the correct process. It was a challenge for Ligne Roset to put my Energia vases into production, however, because the glass is hand-blown, each vase is unique.

The present and future of my field excite me, as increased design coverage in magazines and on television have opened many doors in the industry. People have become more aware of style and design, which has given them the courage to try new things. As a result, products for the

5

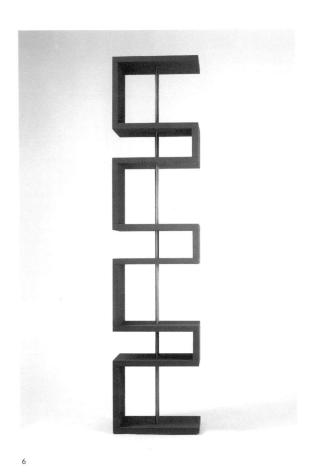

6

7

home are increasingly modern and unique. I believe the future holds even greater opportunities in design and in the integration of art and design.

Today in a field that has long been dominated by male designers, more women are demonstrating their talent. Women will have to persevere to gain equal ground with men. I am proud and inspired by my female colleagues, as we have come a long way. With our confidence as a means, our journey will take us toward further equality in the design field.

5. Energia vase, 2003. Glass, metal. Produced by Ligne Roset.

6. Zigzag shelf, 2002. Wood, metal.

7. Tuba lamp, 2003. Glass, metal. Produced by Ligne Roset.

8. Ice Cube light, 2001. Glass, silicone.

8

The Dish from an Editor
DOWN WITH THE COUNT
Julie Lasky

The idea had been simmering for months: fifty American states, each represented by a single designer. It seemed like an irresistible theme for *I.D.* magazine's fiftieth anniversary in 2004, and somehow my staff and writers pulled it off, scouring the Great Plains, the Sun Belt, and the Hawaiian tropics for talented designers of every stripe.

The issue had been out only a couple of weeks, and I was roaming around web logs, eavesdropping on conversations about it. Almost the first thing I encountered, of course, was The Count. I had been expecting it. I had done everything in my power to fend it off, but there was no stopping it. "Fifty designers, but only six women if you don't include couples," someone pointed out. "Well at least there's progress," came a rejoinder. "A while ago it would have been fifty men, and they all would have been from New York."

The Count is both a symptom of our enlightened culture and a sign that we still have far to go. A few decades ago, no one would have dreamed of scanning a list of speakers at a design conference for signs of female participation, or of toting up percentages of award winners along the XX/XY divide. Few women delivered talks or carried off prizes in those days. In the future, perhaps, anger at the unequal distribution of professional honors, including the honor of being featured in the press, will disappear, not because people will stop caring, but because they will no longer have a reason to fret. For now, I am both relieved and alarmed to report that plenty of numbers are being crunched, plenty of fingers are pointing. "You have a significant responsibility as editor of this magazine—a voice that reaches so many people—to represent all diversities," an industrial design student from Canada chided me after performing The Count on *I.D.*'s Q&A column (only three of the past fourteen interview subjects had been women, she noted). "I hope you understand the need for role models for all of us aspiring designers and professionals."

I do understand. Although half of my correspondent's classmates are female, these women will lose visibility as they ascend the ranks of industrial design, growing wispier and paler in numbers and prestige until, as a group, they will resemble the consumptive wraiths of Victorian novels. Those who stick with their careers, despite the competing demands of domestic life and the skepticism of both employers who fail to promote them and clients who never quite trust them, will join their sisters in other disciplines on the executive sidelines. If you think the cloak of prestige falls any differently in interior design, a field that is more than eighty percent female, I can assure you it does not. Forget Elsie de Wolfe and Eileen Gray, I did my own count several years ago when I edited the now-defunct *Interiors* magazine and discovered that in the twenty-year history of two prestigious awards programs, the Interiors Awards my magazine sponsored and the Interior Design Hall of Fame launched by a competitor, only eighteen percent of the honorees (who received a great deal of press coverage as part of the distinction) were women.

This disparity is not because the media and awards shows are run by men showing preferential treatment toward their own. For as long as women have been slighted in the design industries they have also held powerful jobs in design journalism. Two women, Jane Thompson and Deborah Allen launched *I.D.* (or *Industrial Design*, as it was first known in 1954). Later, the magazine boasted two female chief editors—Annetta Hanna and Chee Pearlman—in a succession that lasted more than a decade. The late *Interiors*, *I.D.*'s sister

publication (I use the phrase pointedly), was headed by Olga Gueft in the 1950s and 1960s and later enjoyed a long and prosperous run under the indomitable Beverly Russell. Among the junior editors who passed through *Interiors* on their way to distinguished careers, Susan Szenasy went on to found *Metropolis*, where she nurtured the career of Karrie Jacobs, who later became founding editor of the architectural magazine *Dwell*, whose current editor is Allison Arieff. *Dwell* is also the rare magazine to be bankrolled by a woman, Lara Hedberg Deam. Women are at the helm of *Architectural Digest*, *House & Garden*, *Real Simple*, *Budget Living*, the *New York Times* style section, and countless other shelter and lifestyle publications. And they are at industry magazines as well. Kristina Goodrich, the executive director of the Industrial Designers Society of America (IDSA), edited the organization's house publication, *Innovations*, for twenty years before recently passing the baton to Mark Dziersk. I have not even mentioned Martha Stewart. What more do I need to say?

Perhaps I should say something about the responsibility of women editors to promote their own. It never feels quite right. One has to fight the perception that one is lowering standards to advance the careers of female practitioners, even when that is emphatically not the case. Or one is accused of condescending to people with ovaries by qualifying their job titles; I once published an issue of *Interiors* devoted entirely to women but then faced the charge of putting my subjects in a ghetto. "We're designers," almost every one of them said. "We just happen to be women, too."

Nonetheless, I found myself staring at a white board where the cast of fifty American designers was being assembled for *I.D.* We were halfway through the process, and men were outnumbering women five to one—and we were counting members of male/female partnerships. "More girls," I insisted, and my colleagues and I pushed harder to find them. Never forsaking our goal—to single out subjects who reflected something distinctive about their regions and whose accomplishments left no question that they belonged in the issue—we found relatively few women in sparsely populated states. Many more of course resided in large cultural centers on either coast, but so did many more men, and the stakes for accomplishment were higher. Who would you pick as the sole design representative of New York State? After much agony we chose someone involved with preserving and constructing several buildings indelibly connected to Manhattan, including the Freedom Tower planned at Ground Zero. He happened to be a man: David Childs of Skidmore, Owings & Merrill.

Why must we still do The Count? Where are all the women who enroll in industrial design and architecture programs in equal or greater numbers than men and should be easy editorial fodder? I am told they get intimidated by male peers, discouraged by potential employers, enticed by related jobs in research and marketing, wrapped up in marriage and child-rearing, shut out of male bastions such as automotive design, blocked by glass ceilings, and funneled into the world of craft with smaller overheads, less politicking, and operations that can be run from home. Even Kristina Goodrich of the IDSA would not commit to a theory. She hopes to initiate a study that can pin down some answers.

By the same token, I asked Jane Thompson, the founding co-editor of *I.D.* fifty years ago, why she and her female colleagues were given such extraordinary opportunities in such a sexist age. "I think it's because our boss, Charlie Whitney, thought he could push us around," she said. Today she is the president of Thompson Design Group in Boston, a practice she shared for thirty-five years with her late husband, Benjamin Thompson. Her job is to revitalize cities, and, like several of my predecessors who possess a variety of chromosomal combinations, she has left an enormous pair of shoes to fill. To refer to her as a "woman" anything would indeed dislodge her from her position in the design world. It has room for only one, and who can argue with that number? We should all be so fortunate as to claim it.

Julie Lasky is editor-in-chief of I.D., *the international design magazine, and former editor of* Interiors *magazine. A widely published writer and critic, she has contributed to the* New York

Times *and numerous design publications, and is the author of*
Borrowed Design: Use and Abuse of Historical Form *(written
with Steven Heller) and* Some People Can't Surf: The Graphic
Design of Art Chantry. *In 1995–6 she was a National Arts
Journalism Program Fellow at the Medill School of Journalism
at Northwestern University. In 1997 she won the Richard J.
Margolis Award for nonfiction writing that demonstrates warmth,
humor, and a concern for social issues. Lasky has lectured on
design from Salt Lake City to Sarajevo.*

1

1. Glory light blanket, 1999.
Silicone rubber, optic fibers.

2. Streol chair, 2001. Rubber,
metal.

Anette Heimann
planA

Born:
Svendborg, Denmark

Practice:
Copenhagen, Denmark and Durban, South Africa

My work is a mixture of functionality, quality, and enough—"enough" as a result of necessity, not as a result of a forced minimum. I do not search for less; I search for that which is needed.

My creative process is hermeneutic. It is a circular process. I search life from detail to entirety, from entirety to detail. This method of introspection and interpretation raises theories that I examine and apply to my own life and work.

Becoming a designer was an incident in the

2

same kind of circular process. I am a curious person. I twist and turn every new object in my path, like a detective searching for evidence. Everything inspires me.

     Designing is like reading a book that will never end; it is about making objects for people to create their own stories. Good design gives you something, an emotion of some sort, each time you look at it or use it. The summation of these feelings and experiences is the creation of your own story with the object. *The "design" of a product does not end*

when the consumer takes it in his home, but rather develops as it lives on in another context.

3

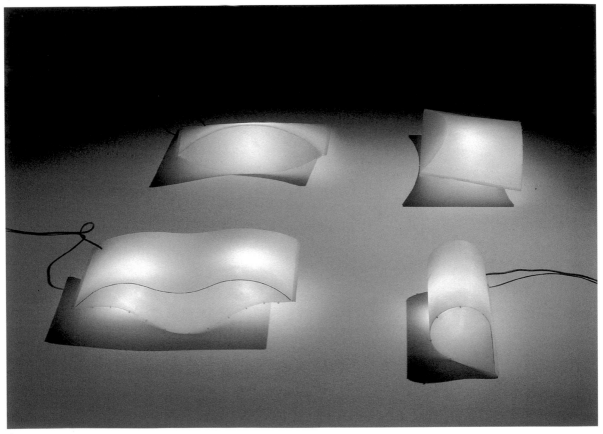

4

3. Baseone 1 and Baseone 3, living room installation, 2001. Three elements to sit or lie upon, image projector.

4. Light pillows, 2000. Polypropylene, electrical parts.

5. Plywood chair, 1995. Plywood, bolts.

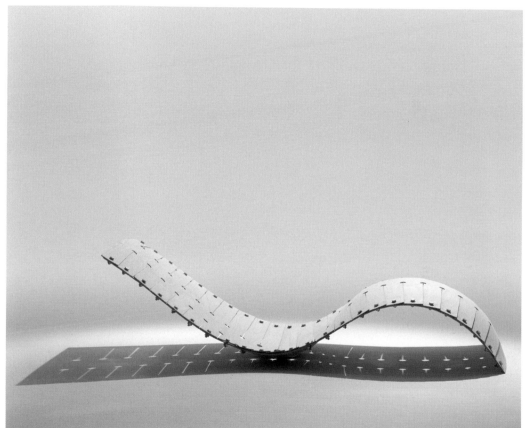

5

1

Dejana Kabiljo

Kabiljo Inc.

Being a designer is such a luxury. I feel privileged to wake up in the morning to a day of ideas, color, shape, and shade. However, the economics of the design business mean there is hardly a chance of my ever becoming too proud.

Being an amateur anthropologist, my passion is the reality of life. I enjoy observing people and their habits: the way they sit, eat, shop, dance, make a mess, and tidy up again. As a voyeur, I secretly take

Born:
Split, Croatia

Practice:
Vienna, Austria

2

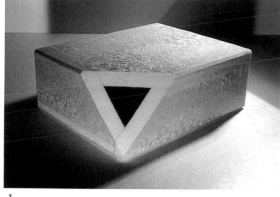

3

3. Procrastination box, 2002.
Biedermeier-patterned Styrofoam,
epoxy resin.

1 and 4. SCRIBOman paper table,
2001. Paper, acrylic.

2. Lim chair, 1990. Aluminum sheet,
wood. Produced by Molteni &
Molteni.

4

photos and videos of their everyday activities in order to go back home and seek out another kind of reality—one that will take their bad habits, little fetishes, and compulsive mannerisms into consideration. Through my design I create an outlet for these behavioral patterns, with the primary goal of bringing pleasure to them.

I enjoy having my own production label, Kabiljo Inc., immensely. Objects and projects come out of our imaginations, hands, and hearts like warm cookies out of an oven. We enjoy creating simple things for our complex times, things that are nice, irony-free, and quite celebratory.

1

1. Relax side table and lamp, 2001. Phenolic resin, metal frame, wood laminate. Produced by FontanaArte.

2. Liquids glasses, 2001. Crystal. Produced by Decorum.

3. Medusa fruit bowl, 1993. Sheet glass. Produced by RSVP.

Defne Koz
Defne Koz Design Studio

Born:
Ankara, Turkey

Practice:
Milan, Italy and Boston, USA

I am a Turkish designer and divide my time between Italy and the United States. I work with companies in Germany, Italy, Japan, and Turkey. Even as I design for international companies, I still feel I am a Turkish designer in Italy because both cultures are the main influences on my work. Turkish culture is my roots. Even if I never refer directly to Turkish design, I feel it. I am fascinated by the history and tradition of Turkey's material culture, which is so original, ancient, and diverse. I try to continue to discover it, and am always happy

2

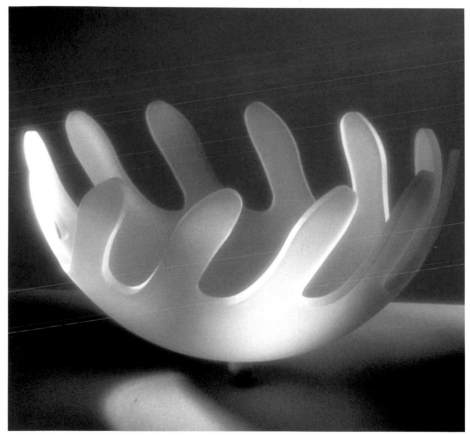

3

when I work with materials that are part of this history, such as glass, ceramics, and textiles. I believe this sensitivity to history is particularly valuable when I work on high-tech projects for industrial production.

I studied and started my design career in Italy. I have learned a lot, in both professional and interpersonal terms, from working there with Ettore Sottsass. Two aspects of his work that I greatly admire are his abilities to think beyond the conventional and to understand life and people. He always surprises me with his ideas.

In his work he constantly searches for meaning, rather than creativity for creativity's sake.

I see design as part of everyday life. I detest design when presented as an elitist style, or, even worse, as the vulgarization of an elitist style. Rather, *design is about what people do every day. It is about the tools people use every day. And it is about adding quality to what people do every day.* I hate to think that something I designed

4

5

could remain on a shelf as decoration. The ideal object is the one you adopt and use every day, and the one that continues to surprise and excite you every time you use it.

I do not understand, or really appreciate, specialization. I do not think a designer should be focused on a single category of products. It is true that some things, like cars and computers, need a specific understanding of complex technical issues, but I feel it is more important to cross-fertilize ideas by working on different products. After all, we designers have only one specialization: understanding how people live with objects, how tools and spaces can change and influence life.

Design is a combination of craftsmanship and industry. There is an artisanal dimension in the way I conceive and develop projects, but I believe my best results emerge out of the craft dimension and become

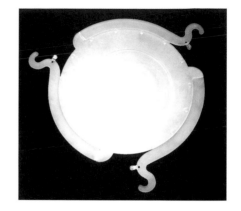

6

4. Medusa tire, 1997. Graphic design for truck tires. Produced by Pirelli.

5. Diogene lamp, 2001. Phenolic resin, electrical parts. Produced by FontanaArte.

6. Aski foldable tray, 1993. Polypropylene. Produced for Neste Form Design Contest.

7. Nest fruit basket, 2001. Mirror-polished stainless steel wire. Produced by Alessi.

7

true industrial products. My wire basket for Alessi, for example, started as an experiment of giving volume to steel wire. When Alessi decided to produce it, we made changes to optimize it for industrial production. Even though it took more than a year to go from first sketches to completion, and many details were changed along the way, it still looks fresh to me.

8. Lady K washbasin, 2000. Resin.
Produced by Rapsel.

9. Tomo sofa, 1994. Upholstery,
wood frame. Produced by Alparda.

10. Touch tiles, 2000. Embossed
ceramic. Produced by Vitra–
Eczaçibasž.

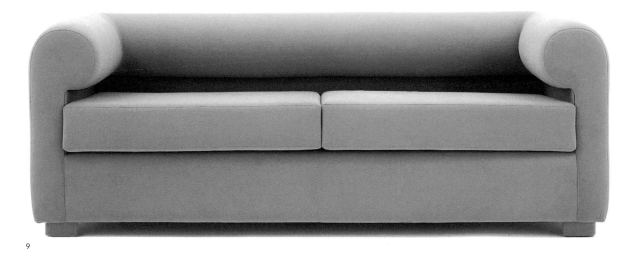

9

10

1

2

Catherina Lande

Born:
Oslo, Norway

Practice:
Oslo, Norway

When I looked for something and could not find exactly what I had in mind, I altered an existing piece or, not wanting to settle with what I found, I tried to make it myself. Filling gaps that in my eyes were missing inspired me to learn more about how to make things. I am motivated by a desire for a quality of life not defined by the accumulation of things, but rather by establishing what is fundamental. I want to contribute to an appreciation and understanding of the essence of life.

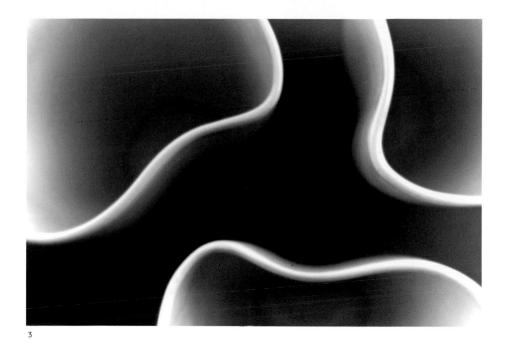

3

4

Quite early in my career, while living in Norway, I started making my own clothes, and then I went to Milan to study fashion design. After spending about seven years there, including being responsible for the women's wear collections of Japanese fashion designer Giuliano Fujiwara, I returned to Norway. I still wanted to learn more, and so I studied product design in Norway and then industrial design in the United Kingdom.

I find working with ordinary objects that we use everyday very challenging. We take these tools for granted and use them all the time without considering why they are as they are or that somebody has spent time giving them their form. They are the invisible tools of everyday life. *Coming from fashion design, I wanted to make something that would last longer than just one season, something one would look after and pass on to the next generation.* The object should fulfill a purpose, not just create a need for the latest fashion.

5

The hands and how we use them are often the starting point for my designs. My goal is that the pieces I make feel as good in the hands as they look to the eyes. Objects related to preparing, serving, and enjoying food in order to turn everyday moments into something special have been my main focus. These unglazed ceramic objects maintain their natural color so that the food or liquid filling them gives them an extra dimension. More recently I have been working in glass and anodized aluminum and enjoying the bright colors that seem so natural in these media.

5 and 6. Futura vases, 2003.
Blown glass. Produced by Magnor
Glassverk AS.

7. Cosmo bowls and Coro tray, 2002.
Aluminum.

6

7

1

2

In all my works, I combine Eastern and Western, modern and traditional, industrial and hand-made, masculine and feminine, natural and synthetic. Since 1999 I have explored new tactile materials for soft furniture, installations, and fashion. It is the visual and tactile characteristics of the materials and textures that stimulate my product ideas.

I am an artist caught between different fields. By mixing techniques, I blur the lines between the applied

Born:
Tehran, Iran

Practice:
Paris, France

1. Etna lamps, 2002. Polyester, electrical parts.

2. Tender place mats, 2000. Synthetic felt of polyester and acrylic.

3. Yek-O-Yek stools, 2002. Wool felt, dense foam.

3

arts, visual arts, and industrial design. It is neither the object itself nor the technical means used to produce it that most interests me, but the feeling and sensation conveyed through the object. Therefore my way of seeing combined with my knowledge can be translated through various media.

Observe, touch, breathe, experiment, go a different way, go beyond technical obstacles. Reinvent things in a way unlike anyone else. Welcome to my poetic and playful world.

1

Ilaria Marelli

Born:
Erba, Italy

Practice:
Milan, Italy

Design came into my life slowly. I had always wondered why there were so many things that expressed a lack of care, and I had always dreamed of doing something that could add a bit of poetry and a touch of irony to people's lives. But it could have been music, or photography, or theater, or architecture. Just recently, I turned to design and have found this approach full of opportunity. Through my work I try to express a new way to look at ordinary objects by merging their positive qualities with something new—a new gesture I have noticed, a

2

3

1. Lucciolo table, 2004. Pleíxiglas, fluorescent pigments. Designed with Diana Eugeni. Produced by Zanotta SpA.

2. Cannot side table, 1999. Stainless steel structure, lacquered top. Designed with Michela Catalano. Produced by Cappellini.

3. Frame CD wall rack, 2001. Anodized aluminum. Produced here by Cappellini. Currently produced by Duepuntosette.

new technology, a new material, or a new combination of all these things.

My ideas come mainly out of listening to the often-unexpressed desires of people, their expectations from relationships, environments, and tools. I combine these with the goals of the producers: commercial potentials, interests, visions, knowledge, and technical or managerial competencies. Often I feel I am a link between the world of production and the everyday lives of all of us. Design creates these relationships; I find a fascination in that and I feel a responsibility to it.

Some of my projects are experimental while others are more conducive to the current market. The course of a project does not derive from a defined strategy, but rather takes shape throughout the research and development process in relation to people I meet and experiences I have. *I usually refer to each of my projects as a creature, a thing living that rises from me and grows with everyone that*

4

5

likes it, produces it, sells it, and uses it. It is always exciting to imagine this connection between me and people I have never met.

I think there is a female sensibility and creativity —a different feeling for relationships, the environment, and the care of things. I cannot imagine the movies of Sally Potter or the performances of Laurie Anderson conceived in the same way by a male brain. Of course, a male culture still dominates many design fields and its influence is prevalent. Nevertheless, the present time offers an exceptional laboratory of cultural and social mixing, local and global sharing of influences, and technological evolution. These factors are influencing the design field, opening questions about what and how to design, and making us think about what we can contribute to increase the beauty and the friendliness of things that surround us.

4. Materia tables, 2002. Ceramic. Designed with Michela Catalano. Produced by Bosa Ceramiche.

5. Apple low table, 2002. Sanded Plexiglas, polyethylene. Produced here by Cappellini. Currently self-produced.

6. Ara floor lamp, 2003. Painted and anodized metal, electrical parts. Produced by Nemo Italianaluce, Cassina Group.

6

1

2

1. Cygnet picnic table, 2003. Solid walnut, aluminum.

2. Bow table, 2003. Steel top, solid pine, 800 lbs. of magnets.

3. Honey shelving, 2003. Aluminum, Knoll fabric.

Ruby Metzner
Hivemindesign

Born:
New York, USA

Practice:
Brooklyn, USA

Growing up in the creative environment of New York, I was encouraged by artists and designers at home and at school to pursue a creative career. I went to college at the Rhode Island School of Design intending to pursue studies in fine art and jewelry. The industrial design department had the best shop facilities and I found myself spending my time there spurred by a simple goal: to learn how to make objects well.

After working for a prominent industrial designer, drafting and outsourcing every one of my ideas, I felt I

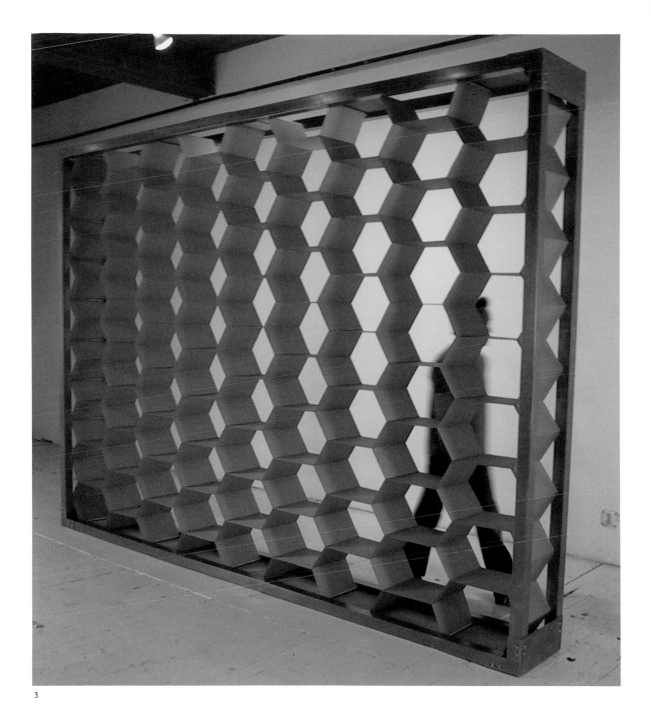

3

needed to go back to the process of making objects myself. In 2000 my partner Sather Duke and I founded Hivemindesign as a consulting design team and manufacturer of interiors, furniture, packaging, and products. We design what we can build, use materials and processes from local sources, and finance our own prototypes. Our location in the industrial center of Brooklyn allows us to outsource to a wide range of fabricators. *Setting up a shop of this kind has set parameters that*

help me focus my ideas.

After having my own business for some years now, I realize that my furniture and products have started to have their own dialogue with each other. I build objects to fulfill my curiosity and try to answer questions that my environment presents me. Design can revolve around necessity, trends, and emerging technologies. My wish is to design work that is visually and physically durable. I would like to see things we have made being used many years from now.

1

Designed by the Emiliana Design Studio. Produced by Nanimarquína.

1. Pillow Play, 1999. Lycra mesh, Styrofoam beads. Produced by Nanimarquína.

2. Sweet Love edible jewelry, 2003. Candy.

3. Flying carpet, 2002. Wool.

Ana Mir

Emiliana Design Studio

Born:
Valencia, Spain

Practice:
Barcelona, Spain

I became a designer because of an ideal: design's apparent ability to reach a very wide public through the interaction of objects seemed to be a very democratic discipline. I see industrial design as a tool for communication, and I seek to exploit it in this way.

As an industrial designer as well as a fine artist, I find that the advantage of mass production—high technology, wide distribution, and low price points—do not make up for the inherent conceptual limitations. Mass-produced products are not allowed to be risky.

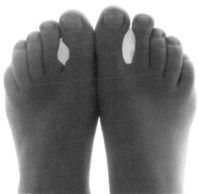

2

3

This results in their being obvious, conventional, and conservative. Even though the process of making a self-produced product may be simple and low-tech, it has the possibility of being a powerful conceptual piece. The disadvantage is its tendency to be more expensive and, sadly, more exclusive.

For me, industrial design is like a second skin. *I am specifically interested in objects and materials that are in direct contact with the body.* For this

reason, I highly value and consider an object's sensual qualities. I am fascinated with the public's reaction when faced with these objects or materials, which affect not only sight but all the senses. Seeking to expand people's relationships to design, I subvert the associations they have with the objects that surround them and create a new situation that expands the boundaries established by culture or society.

Today's women know what they want. As designers, we have created our own language and

4

7. Chocolate Nipples, 1995. Dark chocolates. Produced by chocolatier, Enric Rovira.

4. Hairlace necklace, 1995. Human hair.

5. Tampon Dedo, 1994. Cotton.

6. Hair Disguiser bathroom tiles, 1994. Ceramic. Produced by H2O Gallery.

communicate with one another through our work.
This exchange will inevitably lead to new, progressive
approaches in the industry.

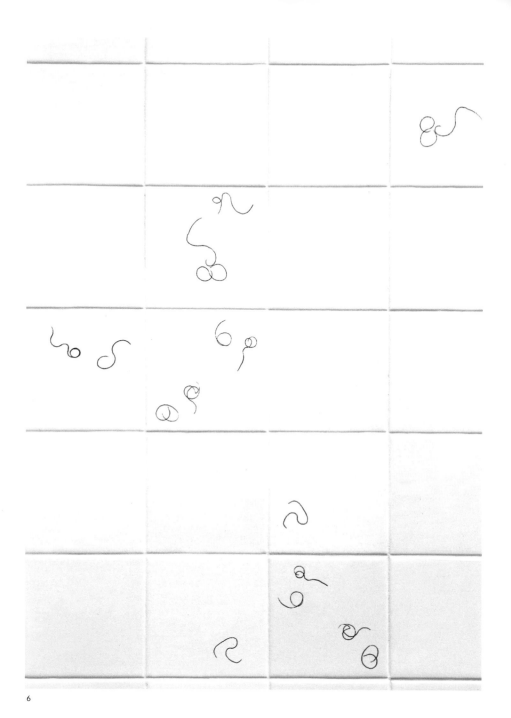

6

7

The Dish from a Design Theorist

THE DIFFERENCE OF FEMALE DESIGN

Hazel Clark

Giving recognition, duly deserved, to the output of women designers begs an important question: do women design differently? And, if so, how? By what processes? Through what impulses? Do women practice design as a subtly different activity from the men who dominate the profession? These are difficult questions, not the least for women designers, especially if they do not necessarily want to be thought of as women designers, but rather as designers who happen to be women. But the publication of *Dish* by its very nature draws attention to the questions.

It remains a fact that even in the twenty-first century, with some exceptions, design is still a largely male-dominated profession (even though the majority of design students in the United States are female). Women tend to be more active in certain areas of design practice than in others, notably design for the home (including furnishings and textiles), and design related to the body (including clothing, accessories, and jewelry). But at the same time women designers remain cautious about promoting their gender. Why is this? Perhaps it is because when the female (the biological given) is expressed as the feminine (the culturally acquired characteristics associated with womanhood), it carries an implicit association with triviality and passivity.

Design emerged as a profession in the early twentieth century at the same time that modernism was developing. Modernism was predicated on polarized binary oppositions where the masculine was always superior to the feminine: rationality over intuition, culture over nature, function over decoration, progress over tradition, public over private, production over consumption, and design over taste equated male over female. In the late twentieth century new ways of thinking and acting, which we now often describe as postmodern, enabled a distancing from these binary equations—an embracing of gender and cultural diversity—and paved the way for the proper acknowledgment and valuing of difference. But this was not difference in the sense of "other," as the alien or the inferior (almost the only ways in which difference could previously be thought). It was difference in its true sense, where what is other is recognized and accepted affirmatively on its own terms.

Today we should have reached the point of being able to respect the talent of women designers and what they offer to design—but have we? Much has changed and continues to change. But the question of how much female difference is actually incorporated into what is, inevitably if unconsciously, a male design canon still remains. Will design produced by women continue to be treated less seriously than that produced by men? Is it to be marginalized as somehow not quite design? The difficulty of negotiating this impasse raises a dilemma for women designers in declaring their gender and identity. But in searching for answers we must be wary of reinforcing the old binary stereotypes. If the work in *Dish* strikes us as different it cannot simply be because of some essentialist notion of "female" or of the "feminine." We must rather look at the work for what it offers and consider both what the designers choose to address and how they do so.

First, there are a series of factors in considering what is addressed. The most central is an attention to context and use and the way that the object is seen as an interface between people and their wants and needs. This includes designs that address exclusively female experience. The most literal example is Ana Mir's tampon —a witty acknowledgement of how an anonymous yet indispensable object can warrant redesign. Mir's Hair

Distinguisher bathroom tiles and Nicolette Brunklaus' Blonde printed textile similarly recognize the female body as women experience it—as visceral and transitory —rather than as objectified in much contemporary design and advertising. The experiential is often missing from design, which tends to instead rely on the visual for its impact. *Dish* develops our understanding of what design might be about when initiated by women's experience.

The experience of some of *Dish*'s designers is that of motherhood, and a number of the designs are for children: Sophie Demenge's Oeuf products for babies, Jennifer Carpenter's Truck furniture, and Laurene Leon Boym's animal rugs, designed originally for her son. Not just miniaturized adult designs, these objects originate from the actual experience of having children. Becoming mothers has contributed to expanding some women's concerns as designers.[1] Family has made a difference to these women as it has for their creative predecessors. Famously, the patchwork quilt that Sonia Delaunay made for her son's crib marked her highly successful move from painting to designing textiles.

Design for the home provides the core focus for *Dish*, but if women designers do have a stronger relationship to the home than their male counterparts, it is one that is defined more by social and cultural practice than by biology. The designs demonstrate an empathy with context and use. The rugs, textiles, furniture, and objects in *Dish* are largely one-of-a-kind, functional but not functionalist. Many provide sensory pleasure and humor and invite participation. Louise Campbell's SeeSaw and Dejana Kabiljo's SCRIBOman table are forms that demand use. Lily Latifi's felt and foam stools and felt mats call for reconfiguration by the user. Much of the work draws upon an understanding of our wants and needs from our homes—the practical, but also the comforting, the relaxing, the sensual, and the playful. Of course some of the designs—Patricia Urquiola's furniture, for example—do not appear to allude to "women's work" at all but still retain a high level of sensitivity toward the user.

The designs draw our attention to the everyday. Experiences that might otherwise be ignored or considered mundane—the simple act of eating, for example—are highlighted and reevaluated. Catherina Lande's Munyal porcelain plates are utilitarian and explore tactile as well as visual qualities; she calls them "the invisible tools of everyday life," and as such they help celebrate the fundamental human activity of eating.

Recognizing that home is a place of consumption highlights design's social responsibility; in the process of using we need also to be aware of what is used-up and what is left over. Inna Alesina's Good Egg footstool, made from post-consumer paper egg crates, is part of a product line she has designed and manufactured from recycled materials. Monica

Nicoletti's Place Holder cardboard moving boxes are embellished with images that can both reflect their contents and allow them to serve as temporary furniture—thus challenging conventions of what is to be consumed and what is permanent.

Many of *Dish*'s designers not only design for the home but also work at home, often collaboratively with male domestic partners or with other women. A preoccupation with human relationships characterizes their working methods as much as what they design. A number of the designers are committed to education; in teaching and promoting design they give support to students and younger designers. The how of what they choose to do is as much a consideration as the what—this is evident in their processes, techniques, and materials.

Some of the designs herein reference the traditionally feminine areas of design in innovative ways. Textiles, for instance, are not only superficially designed in color and pattern; their material traits are also explored. Lauren Moriarty takes thread and weaving as the point of departure for her three-dimensional products and cut neoprene fabrics. The decorative is explored, but not merely as an application, as an implied outcome of feminine leisure activity. In Elizabeth's Chandelier designed by Lyn Godley, for example, the decorative is fully integrated with the product.

This lamp is characteristic of the work in *Dish*, many of which are prototypes or one-offs that suggest the hand-made. This is often a deceit, with products such as Moriarty's textiles deriving from highly sophisticated technological processes. But the designs are not rhetorically technological—technology does not become a barrier between the thing and the user as it does with so many contemporary designs.

This collection begins to redress the binary opposition of modernism, not only for women designers but also for design itself. By restating the ways that design acts as an interface between people and their activities, experiences, needs, and desires, *Dish* brings a different voice to design—different but no less equal.

1 Jane Margolies, "Getting Tough About Kids' Stuff: Four Designing Mothers Sound Off on Baby Products," *I.D.*, March/ April 2004, 42–9.

Hazel Clark has a PhD in the history of design. Her research and writing has encompassed design history and theory, with a particular interest in fashion, textiles, and designed artifacts. She is chair of the Department of Critical Studies at Parsons School of Design, New York, and she was previously head of the Swire School of Design, Hong Kong Polytechnic. She is the editor of Design Issues *19:3 (2003) on design in Hong Kong, author of* The Cheongsam *(2000), and co-editor of* Old Clothes, New Looks: Second Hand Dress *(2004).*

3. Anatomy series: Gluteus Maximus-
Big Rose Muscle, Gluteus Maximus-
Big Black Muscle, and Corpus-Rose
Body, 2001. Murano glass. Produced
by Covo.

1. Barnacle wall tiles and towel
hooks, 2000. Earthenware ceramic.

2. Zero swivel chair, 2002. Foam
upholstery, chrome or steel base.
Produced by Offecct.

Marre Moerel

Marre Moerel Design
Studio

Born:
Breda, The Netherlands

Practice:
Madrid, Spain

Because I have moved to different countries over the years and adapted to different cultures, my immediate surroundings are my main source of design inspiration. I have always been fascinated by what people surround themselves with and how it reflects their lifestyle and beliefs.

My focus is creating objects that challenge the way we live and readdress accepted norms. To me, an important aspect of design is the emotional connection developed over time between the object and the user. Through my work I try to question the value of the emo-

2

3

tional versus the physical and to provoke a psychological reaction, rather than create a merely functional tool. To accentuate my ideas I use found objects or existing shapes. *I like to adopt highly recognizable forms by putting them in a different and unusual context.* In that way, I create a new language that can easily be understood, while still commenting on the old one.

My work is an evolving story. It is an expression of related ideas and concepts, rather than individually designed pieces. I try to accentuate this through simplicity and repetition in form, color, and material. By pushing the boundaries of form and material through experimentation, the user hopefully becomes more aware and engaged with the objects. The designs become truly active pieces with a life and character of their own, ultimately providing a physical, as well as spiritual, engagement.

I work alone in my studio, which has a very basic setup of the tools necessary to make

4

prototypes. I prefer to develop pieces by myself, without the economic and time constraints of the manufacturing industry. This allows me to work at my own pace and let the objects "grow" into being. I tend not to make drawings, but start straight on full-scale models with a vague notion of what the thing is going to be. Through the process of adding and changing, the object starts to take shape. This hands-on design process, which perhaps is laborious and not the most cost-effective, allows for things to happen that could not be anticipated on

paper or computer. And, for me, the three-dimensional process of making models is a far more personal and therefore satisfying experience.

I believe all designers are different, with their own way of working and expressing themselves, and all have to find a way of making it work for themselves. The only difference between male and female designers (apart from the occasional condescending treatment women receive in the local hardware store, which makes me laugh) is that design done by women possibly has a

5

4. Grow storage unit, 1998.
Painted MDF.

5. Polyp hanging or standing lamp,
2000. Earthenware ceramic, incandescent lighting components.
Produced by Cappellini.

6. Soft Box series, 1999.
Earthenware ceramic, incandescent
lighting components. Produced by
Cappellini.

6

more feminine, softer touch to it. But that seems to be disappearing quickly, as both male and female issues and sensibilities have started to blend. Success or failure in design relies on—besides being good at what you do—what kind of person you are, how well you are able to promote yourself and your work, and how aggressive a salesperson and businessperson you are. But ultimately this is true for any kind of business, and design is no exception.

1

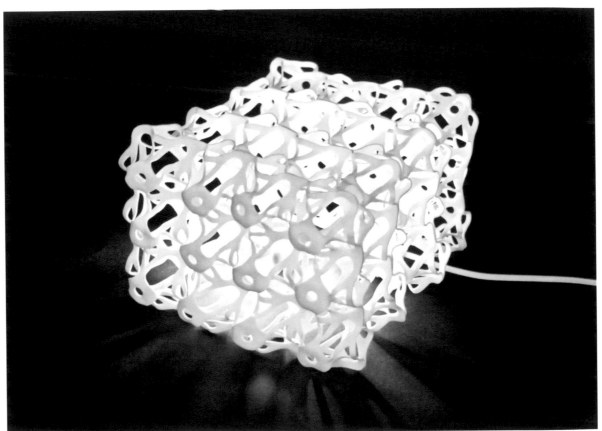

2

Lauren Moriarty

I take a lighthearted approach toward designing products. I think they should sometimes be beauliful and
intricate, sometimes functional and fun, and sometimes
funny and clever. They should bring a bit of enjoyment
to everyday life.

    I have combined my background in textile design
and industrial design to create my own niche. I like to be
surrounded by strong color and interesting textures.
In general, I strive to visually stimulate the viewers and
make them want to touch the work. *And I like*

Born:
Bury St. Edmunds, UK

Practice:
London, UK

1. Rubber Cut fabrics, 2002. Laser-cut neoprene.

2. Noodle Block light, 2001. Laser-cut neoprene, lighting components.

3. Black Lace panel, 2002. Laser-cut neoprene.

3

it when people are puzzled and intrigued by how a piece was constructed.

My designs are currently produced in small batches using a mixture of industrial processes and self-production. My goal is to put some of my designs into mass manufacturing in the future. But I will continue to produce one-off, intricate pieces for gallery displays.

Finding the right material and process to bring a design to life can be challenging but also extremely interesting and enlightening. For the work shown here, I took the traditional technique of lace making and translated it into a contemporary form using modern materials and industrial processes. I made lots of drawings of lace to establish the structure, and then added my own observations and ideas to develop three-dimensional neoprene structures with a lacy look.

As lifestyles change, design will change. I expect to see products that can be carried with the user to create a home away from home.

1

boxes. Produced by Georges Furniture.

1. Reminiscence place mats, 2002. Large format printing on synthetic matting. Produced by Group Inc.

2. Place Holders/Moving Boxes/Transitional Furniture, 2003.. Printed, embellished cardboard

Monica Nicoletti Group Inc.

Born:
Rimini, Italy

Practice:
Milan, Italy and New York, USA

One of the ironies of my passion for design is that I have no idea why I became a designer. Although I was raised in the environment of fashion production, there was not much other creativity in my family. My mother was a seamstress, and I was assigned the odd tasks to assist her in her work. This might have been the catalyst for my own interest in design. As an adolescent I expressed my independence in the way I dressed. The knowledge of tailoring instilled by my mother allowed me to easily transfer my ideas of personal

2

style into custom clothing, fashion design, and ultimately product design.

My work processes personal influences from the media, my cultural history, and my emotional experiences. I have encountered many barriers to my design, some internal and some external. However the largest obstacle is that the elements currently involved in bringing a product from ideation to realization hinder "pure design." To me, design is that instant of eureka; after that, the labor of love begins. Often I find that during the laborious part of the process the essence of the design is affected and undermined. I try to limit my involvement in this portion of the process until I have exhausted all the potential for creativity. In doing this I allow myself to remain unbiased to new ideas and open-minded enough to discover the ironic twists that I strive for in my design.

I see myself as a container of influences, always mentally storing things that touch me

3

emotionally and sensually. The design process begins when I use these influences to develop aesthetic notions. These ideas get applied to design situations and are filtered by my ideals and personal taste. Above all, I think all design must be an example of a designer's good taste. In the end, it is the designer's taste that determines which designs will be proposed as a solution to a problem and whether the design will eventually be universally accepted.

I find that my thoughts on aesthetics are holistic.

As I pursued a career in fashion, I became interested in how fashion influenced music, film, and literature. This cross-pollination led me to appreciate the tangential areas of fashion design and finally to experiment with soft goods through Group Inc. With this collaboration I have the freedom to access diverse resources and design beyond the scope of traditional fashion. This multidisciplinary experience of design has been incredible and has liberated parts of my design psyche that were dormant while designing fashion. Every design is a

4

5

journey of personal discovery, and my development as a
designer relies upon challenging myself to take as many
different journeys as possible along the way.

1

Inga Sempé

Born:
Paris, France

Practice:
Paris, France

I wanted to become a designer because I have always been interested in the objects that surround us daily. An intelligent wall clock or a nice cup moves me more than a piece of art or a church. When looking at a common object, like a spoon or a hammer, I often think of the designer who conceived it and searched for hours for the right curves or combinations of materials, details the user will not necessarily notice. I am charmed by objects that enable me to imagine their conceivers. For all these reasons, I like

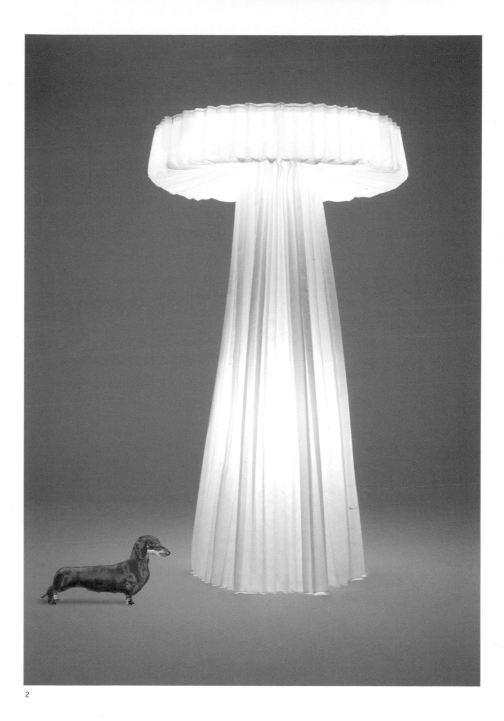

1. View of solo exhibition, Musée des Arts Décoratifs, Paris, 2003.

2. Grande Plissée Lampe, 2002. Pleated synthetic fabric. Produced by Cappellini.

hardware shops and flea markets, not really to buy but to look.

I have never done any self-production because it is another job entirely. I would never be able to rent a corner in a fair, to take the eventual orders, and to securely pack the things while scolding late suppliers. Design is often already complicated in terms of research for materials, fabricators, and distributors.

A typical journalist question is, "From where does your inspiration come," as if it were a tap that opens whenever needed. I appreciate different styles, different minds that might not be close to my own. I admire other designers who do things that I would never be able to do, and I also love those who design exactly how I would dream to do it. But this does not mean they inspire me. *I do not have any inspiration—I mostly feel dry and empty—and the only way for me to be rid of this feeling is to draw.* Although I do not really like to draw, it

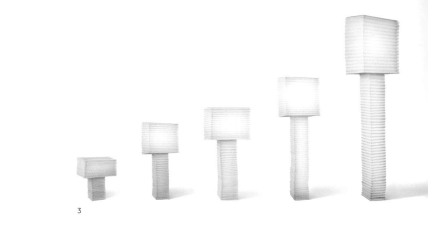

3

4

brings me ideas and solutions. I never draw for any reason except for designing an object. I have to draw and redraw until the project is precisely inscribed in my mind; then I can go to the next step.

I do not feel any advantages in being a woman in the design industry. Nor do I know the changes that may come out of the greater number of women in the industry. But I hope that in a few years, a book about women's design will sound as crazy as a book about men's.

6. Horloge, 2000. Wood, electronic parts. Prototype produced with the support of VIA. Valorisation de l'Innovation dans l'Ameublement. Produced by Ghaadé.

3. Lampe Extensible, 2001. Tearproof paper, lighting components.

4. Chaise metal rembourré (Stuffed Metal Chair), 2003. Metal, neoprene foam rubber, leather, epoxy paint. Produced with the support of VIA,

Valorisation de l'Innovation dans l'Ameublement.

5. Petite, moyenne, grande Lampe Plate, 2004. Steel, plastic, cast iron, lighting components. Produced by Cappellini.

5

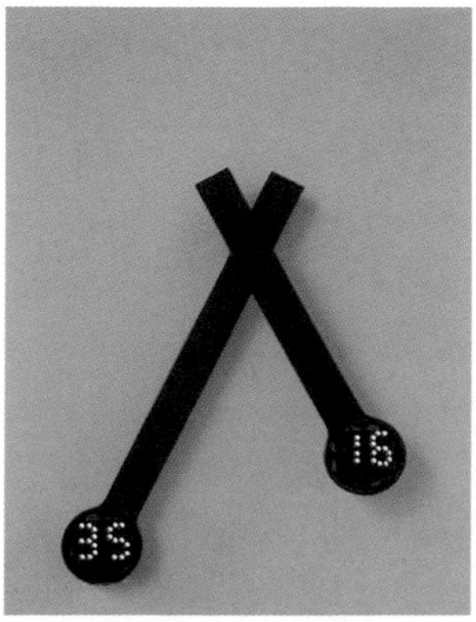

6

Sempé 174/175

1

2

1. Cocoon rocking sofa, 2002. Upholstery, multidensity foam, wood.

2. Kitty Pod, 1998. Corrugated cardboard, maple.

3. Bird cabinet, 2002. Cast resin, high-gloss paint.

Elizabeth Paige Smith

Born:
Houston, USA

Practice:
Los Angeles, USA

When designing an object, a piece of furniture, or an interior, I think of how it can become a stimulant for an experience. There are infinite opportunities to redefine the way objects are perceived and the way they occupy space. My goal is not to create statement pieces, but to achieve a true sensuality of form that naturally attracts and engages the user, evoking desire and curiosity.

I believe it is a designer's responsibility to challenge tradition. By pushing an idealized form into a new landscape, its associations are stripped down and

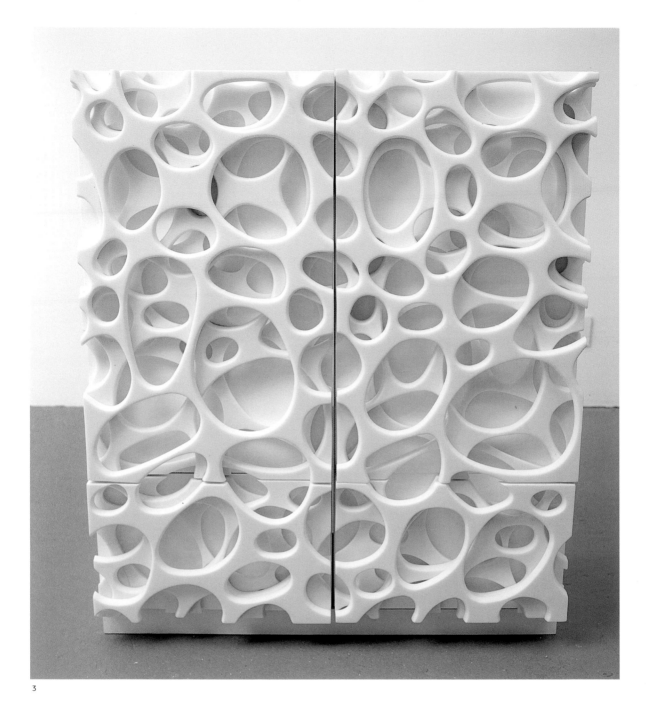

3

reinvented. My process of discovery and reinvention is incorporated with the object's essential functionality and a celebration of nature's subtleties.

I find the workings of nature fascinating and inspiring. *Inspiration may come from a microscopic image, a rock formation, or a lonely insect wing on a windowsill.* It comes from all places. I am interested in creating organic forms using both natural and synthetic materials. Unnatural materials often abstract the natural

form and can challenge our perception of the object's origin.

Other sensory influences, such as sound, stimulate an emotion in me that is communicated directly through my work. Many of the designs I have created recently relate to love, attraction, comfort, and softness, with a major focus on intimacy. Our current environment can be hostile and stressful, inducing a need for warmth and security. My objects communicate visually, offering a sensitivity and a perspective that, I believe, allows one to dream.

4

5

6

lacquer finish.

7. Curve chair, 1998. Resin-coated wood, solid maple.

8. Cube table, 1999. Resin-coated balsa wood.

4. Embrace tête-à-tête, 2002. Acrylic, loose powder pigment.

5. Bleu coffee table, 2000. Resin-coated wood, powder-coated steel.

6. Nude dining chairs with Milk table, 2002. Molded fiberglass,

7

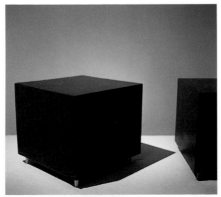

8

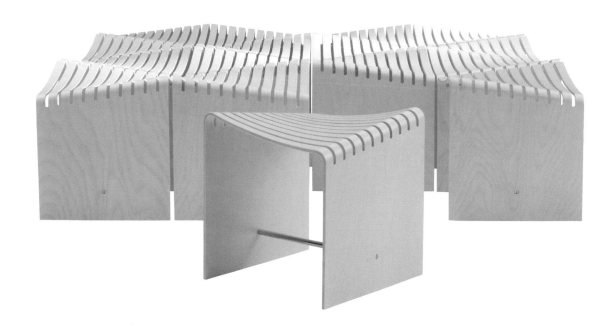

1

Yuriko Takahashi

When I am developing an idea, I promise myself not to be selfish. I like to make my design for the people who will actually use it. I always try to imagine how my piece will be used in someone's life. I think this is the difference between artists and designers. I never disregard the function of my products, but seek a sense of humor and multi-functionality on top of this basic function. Primarily, I want people to find my pieces comfortable, and then to discover a new charm (visually or functionally) within them.

Born:
Narita City, Japan

Practice:
Tokyo, Japan and Copenhagen, Denmark

2

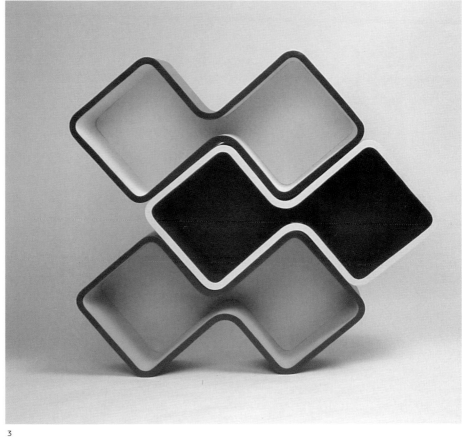

1. Twister stool-bench, 2002. Form-pressed plywood. Produced by Swedese.

2. Seaflower lamp/object, 1999. Plastic.

3. Pea-pod shelf, 2001. Form-pressed plywood.

3

It is a great challenge to design a product for everybody and to keep it unique by proposing a new style. However, I believe it can be done. When I connect with people by offering them ideas for their new lifestyles, I am most encouraged.

As a designer, I have never really been conscious of being a woman. It is like my being Japanese, a part of my identity. Because I am not an artist, I do not specifically try to put my own individuality or history in my work. But I do think that when I am designing, my feminine side, my Japanese mentality, and the rest of my background emerges more or less naturally. This is what I find interesting in being a designer.

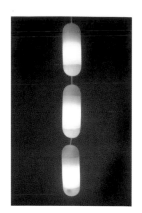

4

4. Sausage light, 2002. Plastic.

5. Dimple table, 2002. Plastic, metal.

6. Jellyfish foldable stool, 1998. Leather.

5

6

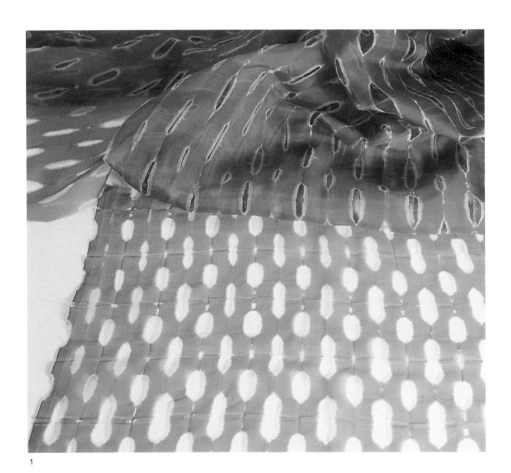

1

1. Sponge, 2003. Chemically etched silk.

2. Copper, 2003. Chemically etched silk.

3. Blue, 2003. Chemically etched silk.

4. Thread, 2003. Chemically etched silk.

Sarah Unruh

Born:
Chattanooga, USA

Practice:
New York, USA

My interest in design began during my first year of art school, when I was introduced to methods of manufacturing common objects. I developed an obsession with the way things were made. I began to look at everyday objects, like plastic trash cans, and imagine the press mold that produced them. I was driven by techniques involving handwork, yet I was fascinated by the consistency and refinement of industrially produced objects.

With this in mind, I started experimenting with processes and forms until something personally

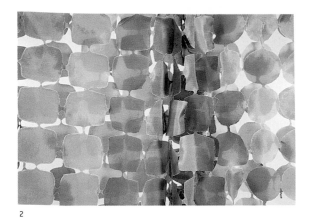

2

3

4

inspiring developed. I created prototypes and finished pieces by hand to look as though they were industrially produced. In this way I developed a series of seating that also functioned as lighting. The light was diffused by fabric, launching me on a path that incorporated patterns of fabric with the use of light and transparency.

My foundation in furniture design forced me to approach the use of fabric in a three-dimensional way. I created pattern through a building process

instead of as an applied decorative surface. I was discovering a way of creating surface patterns from the objects I was making. Out of entanglements of metal, wire, and string came two-dimensional patterns.

In my recent textile work, I have adapted a form of Japanese shibori dying to create patterns that are defined by light and space. Pattern is articulated by spaces that have been etched out of the fabric in a resist-dye bath. The result is a decorative pattern that is a direct consequence of the applied technique. 184/185

1. Void table, 2003. Oak wood, glass. Produced by B&B Italia.

2. Fjord chair system, 2002. HIREK seat-shells, varnished steel frame and beams, polished aluminum feet. Produced by Moroso.

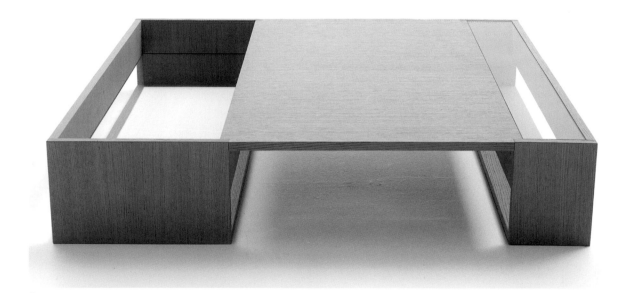

1

Patricia Urquiola
Studio Urquiola

Born:
Oviedo, Spain

Practice:
Milan, Italy

I believe in circumstance. I had studied architecture in Madrid, but moved to Italy to finish my studies at the Politecnico di Milano. There I had an important encounter with Achille Castiglioni, my professor and an internationally renowned master of design. In Spain everyone considered architecture as a major art and design as a minor art. I understood from him that this preconception was wrong, and I found a new passion: industrial design. Design is my instinctive way of expression. It is my obsession.

2

Industrial design is based on the premise that the project be produced in an industrial way. If a form does not apply to this definition, it may be closer to art. Despite its problems and limitations, I feel comfortable with the engineering and manufacturing aspects of the industry. The teamwork essential in design is part of the joy and part of the pain, but at the end of the day the responsibility of the project falls on the designer's shoulders. Compromises are unavoidable, but it is solely up to the designer to decide how many, which ones, and how far to go. *The success of an object is not dependent on the quantity produced, but rather the appropriateness of the production process and the interest it provokes.*

I find that the greatest challenge as a designer is being contemporary while simultaneously creating a language that will defy time. I must be able to visualize the object in the future. It normally takes at least eighteen months from the initial idea to its

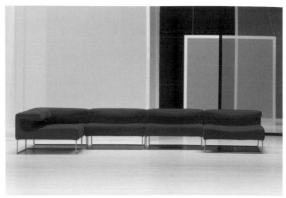

3

4

introduction into the market, and I hope that it will still be interesting several years later. There is a smart architectural prize that only takes buildings into consideration ten years after they are built—that is, in fact, a good time span to provide greater objectivity.

By moving in different directions and fields, I try not to repeat myself in my work. Neither do I seek out the latest technology nor attempt to fill a gap, but instead seek to express the mysterious notions that form inside of me. I desire that all my projects have an

understated message and an inner soul. Above all else, my products must be seductive. The seduction does not have to be in capital letters, but can be expressed in one simple element that captures your emotion.

To be a good designer or a good individual you need a mixture of masculine and feminine traits. With my work I try to communicate what I like and what affects me. I hope people will soon find a more personal way of using what is around them without following any guidelines, mixing more of what the market offers.

3. Lowseat, 2003. Steel frame, polyurethane foam. Produced by Moroso.

4. Malmo, 2002. Steel frame, flame-retardant polyurethane foam, goose down cushions. Produced by Moroso.

5. Fjord Relax chair and ottoman, 2002. Steel frame, flame-retardant foam. Produced by Moroso.

6. Clip bed, 2002. Padded, adjustable headboard, upholstery. Produced by Molteni.

5

6

7

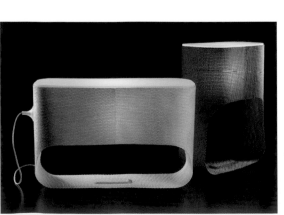

8

7. Sgt. Pepper, 2003. Silver. Produced by De Vecchi.

8. Bague table light, 2003. Colored, silicone-coated metallic net, satinated diffuser. Designed with Eliana Gerotto. Produced by Foscarini.

9. Fat Fat tables, 2002. Fabric, felt, or leather covering, rotational-molded polyethylene frame, polyurethane with flakes of regenerated PET fill, lathe-turned metal cover trays. Produced by B&B Italia.

9

1

1. Clouds bowl, 2001. Glass.
Produced by Kosta Boda.

2. Soapbubble vases, 1999. Glass.
Produced by Kosta Boda.

Ann Wahlstrom

Kosta Boda

Born:
Stockholm, Sweden

Practice:
Stockholm, Sweden

I come from a craft background and used to make my own products in ceramic and glass before I began working In the Swedish glass industry with Kosta Boda. This new job gave me a chance to try different techniques and explore many ideas. It is a very different role—making things with others, as opposed to on your own—but I like being part of this team. I have also done designs in metal, ceramic, and textile for different companies, with everything manufactured industrially.

2

Although designers at glassworks have the
opportunity to work with both experimental, handmade,
one-of-a-kind objects and designs for production, the
former has defined me as a designer. They are two
sides of the same coin, but the exclusive, limited pieces
tend to be more personal. It is amazing that something
so crafted can exist within an industry. In Scandinavia
we refer to this type of industry as *Konstindustri*,
which translates to "art industry." The key is the level of
craftsmanship on all products. When it comes to the

more industrial ideas, I can continue from my handmade
experiments and objects, working them out with
skilled engineers rather than craftsmen. *But it
is the collaboration that makes
the difference; sometimes it works
wonderfully and sometimes it is
difficult to get your idea across, but
it still beats working by yourself.*

I like to alternate between handcrafted products,
one-of-a-kind or small series, and projects

3. Cyklon vase, 2001. Glass.
Produced by Kosta Boda.

4. Nest vases, 2002. Glass.
Produced by Kosta Boda.

5. Spiral bowl, 2001. Glass.
Produced by Kosta Boda.

that bring an idea to a larger product series. The latter usually involves a much longer product development period, and I can get instant gratification by working with handmade objects in the meantime. The challenge as an industrial designer is to be able to compromise but still retain the feeling of your initial idea. This gets more difficult the further into a complicated product development process you get, but keeping your idea as true as possible, and convincing both product developers and production people of the same, is a great reward.

I do not have a specific philosophy behind my work. I design things with which I would like to surround myself. I do not see myself as a female designer, but rather as a creative person who happens to communicate by designing objects. My inspiration is nature on one hand and architecture (old and new) on the other. I have one very "round" organic side and one that is much more clean and precise. My instinct is probably a key element to my work, since it is hard to explain with words when a design feels just right.

4

5

BIOGRAPHIES

Lindsey Adams Adelman
Butter

Lindsey Adams Adelman and David Weeks founded Butter in 2000, creating a line of deceptively simple, well-priced light fixtures. After receiving a degree in industrial design from the Rhode Island School of Design, Adelman worked for Resolute, a lighting company in Seattle, for two years. In 1998 she returned to New York to work with Weeks at his design studio in Brooklyn. Her personal work as well as her work for Butter has since been widely exhibited.

Inna Alesina
Alesina Design

Inna Alesina was born in 1969 in Kharkov, Ukraine. She studied industrial design at the Ukrainian Institute of Industrial Arts and, soon after moving to the United States, continued her studies at Parsons School of Design. Alesina's interest in universal design and environmental issues led her to design products, such as the Wade bathtub seat and the Good Egg footstool, that have won numerous awards and wide recognition by the press. Currently, she teaches industrial design at Towson University, designs furniture for foreign manufacturers, and works as in-house design consultant for a Baltimore-based sports and outdoor products company.

Ayse Birsel
Olive 1:1

Ayse Birsel founded Olive 1:1, a New York-based product design consultancy in 1996. Her clients include Target, Renault, Knoll, and Herman Miller, for whom she designed the Resolve office

Laurene Leon Boym
Boym Partners

Born in New York, Laurene Leon Boym graduated from the School of Visual Arts in 1985, received a masters in industrial design from the Pratt Institute in 1993, and cofounded Boym Partners with her husband, Constantin Boym, in 1994. The studio has designed award-winning products, graphics, and museum exhibitions for an international list of companies including Acme, Alessi, Flos, Swatch, and Vitra. Their work has received numerous design awards and extensive media coverage and has been acquired by most major international museums, including the Museum of Modern Art, New York.

Diana Brennan

Born in Sydney, Australia, Diana Brennan has lived in France since 1974. She studied at the National Art School, Sydney and the Department of Fine Arts, Pantheon-Sorbonne, Paris. Her work has been shown in numerous group and solo exhibitions throughout Europe and Australia and is part of the permanent collections of the Beaux Arts Museum, Beaune in Burgundy, Thomson CSF Versailles, and the Textile Gallery-Museum in Sydney. Brennan has been a teacher at the Ecole Supérieure des Arts Appliqués—Duperé in Paris since 1994.

Nicolette Brunklaus
Nicolette Brunklaus Amsterdam

Born in the Netherlands, Nicolette Brunklaus graduated from the Art Academy Minerva, Groningen, Netherlands in sculpture in 1988. During the following several years she worked as an artist, exhibiting in Italy and the United States, and in 1993 began a brief furniture collaboration with the Dutch artist Lynne Leegte. Brunklaus's work soon began to focus on in several furniture and architectural design firms before founding Lemongras design studio with Moritz Engelbrecht in 1997. Both designers hold a master degree from the Royal College of Art in London. Based in Munich, the studio focuses on furniture and product design as well as interior architecture for hotels and offices.

Jessica Corr

Based in New York, Jessica Corr's projects span a variety of design media: product, retail, museum exhibit, lighting, and set design (in collaboration with Robert Wilson, among others). In 2000 she founded Collabcrative, an interdisciplinary experimental design lab, which has received widespread publicity. Corr received her BFA from Parsons School of Design, where she is currently teaching luminaire design. Her work was featured as part of the 2003 National Design Triennial at the Cooper-Hewitt, National Design Museum..

Matali Crasset
Matali Crasset Productions

After graduating from L'Ecole Nationale Supérieure de Création Industrielle—ENSCI/ Les Ateliers in Paris in 1991, Crasset went to work with Denis Santachiara in Milan and, later, Philippe Starck in Paris. During the five years she worked for Starck, she became the design director of Tim Thom, Thomson Multimedia's design center. In 1998 Crasset founded her own studio. She has been the recipient of numerous award and grants. She has designed products for companies such as Artemide, Domeau & Pérès, Dornbracht, Hermès, and Lexon, interior architecture projects, exhibition design, and most recently, the HI Hotel in Nice, France.

PHOTOGRAPHY CREDITS

Lindsey Adams Adelman
1-6, Bio: Butter

Inna Alesina
1, 4-6: Inna Alesina
2, 3: Gleb Kutepov
Bio: Leonid Guzman

Ayse Birsel
1, 2, 4: Herman Miller
3: Knoll
5, 7, 8: Merati
6: Decorum
Bio: Anne Rochegude

Helena Bodin & Johanna Egnell
1: Söderbergs
2: bodinegnell
3, 4, Bio (Egnell): IKEA/Tina Björeman
5: David Design
Bio (Bodin): Helena Bodin

Sophie Demenge
R+D Design and Oeuf

Sophie Demenge was raised in Paris, France. After studying philosophy at the Sorbonne, she moved to San Francisco and then New York, where she earned her degree in industrial design from the Pratt Institute. In 1999 Michael Ryan joined Demenge to form R+D Design. The firm favors the intimate and the playful, contributing to design with a lightness of heart and appreciation of craftsmanship. In 2003 Demenge and Ryan formed a second company, Oeuf, focusing on furniture and accessories for children.

Florence Doléac

After receiving a degree in visual arts in 1990, Florence Doléac pursued her studies at L'Ecole Nationale Supérieure de Création Industrielle—ENSCI/Les Ateliers in Paris. She was a member of the RADI Designers from 1994 to 2003, where she worked on a range of objects and installations. Since 2000 she has been a teacher in Switzerland at L'ECAL, Ecole Cantonale d'Art de Lausanne. Beginning in December 2002, she has been represented by Galerie Aline Vidal, which has exhibited her work in solo exhibitions.

Rie Egawa
egawa + zbryk

Rie Egawa is a Japan transplant and graduate of Pratt Institute in printmaking. After a stint as a textile designer in the New York fashion industry, Rie founded egawa + zbryk with her husband, Burgess Zbryk, in 1998. Her company has exhibited work internationally. Based in Kansas City, Missouri, the firm was the recipient of a design distinction award in I.D. magazine's 2001 design review and the winner of the IDEE Design Competition, Japan, 2001.

printed images for furniture and textile design. In 2003 Brunklaus was nominated for the prestigious FX award for her Shady Tree light in the category of best residential furniture and lighting.

system, now in the permanent collection of the Museum of Modern Art, New York. Birsel has been the recipient of numerous design awards, including the Cooper-Hewitt National Design Award in 2002, and her work has been extensively published and exhibited throughout the world.

Louise Campbell
Leo Limito

After graduating from the London College of Furniture and returning to Denmark for a master's degree, Campbell founded her own company in 1996. She has since received commissions from several manufacturers, including Erik Jorgensen Møbelfabrik, Bahnsen, and Louis Poulsen Lighting. Campbell was a primary organizer for the exhibition Walk the Plank and was given a solo exhibition at the Trapholt Museum in Denmark. The two venues represent two important trends in her career: commissions from museums and manufacturers and self-generated projects and curatorial exhibitions.

Helena Bodin & Johanna Egnell
bodinegnell

Helena Bodin and Johanna Egnell studied product design at Beckmans School of Design in Sweden. Before opening their own practice in 2000, Bodin was invited to design a unique prototype for Mitsubishi and Egnell worked as a film production designer for Swedish television. Bodinegnell has designed products for David Design, Stockholm Design House, R.O.O.M., Söderbergs Furniture, Asplund, and IKEA of Sweden. Their work also includes both commercial and residential interiors.

Jennifer Carpenter
Truck Product Architecture

Jennifer Carpenter studied art, design, and art history as an undergraduate at Yale. After graduating with a master of architecture from Columbia University, she launched a handbag design and manufacturing business with her husband. In 1999 she became a registered architect and joined Rogers Marvel Architects. In 2001 she founded Truck, a furniture and product design company, with RMA partners Rob Rogers and Jonathan Marvel. Carpenter lives in New York with her husband Dave and baby Booker.

Kelly Bortoluzzi & Kristin Ordahl
Orbo Design

Kelly Bortoluzzi, a graduate of Parsons School of Design in product design, and Kristin Ordahl, a painter and graduate of the Philadelphia College of Art, are the founders of Orbo Design. A three-year-old company based in Brooklyn, New York, Orbo Design has gained widespread recognition for reinventing the canvas rug. Their work is frequently commissioned by prominent architects and clients such Robert A.M. Stern Architects, Shiseido Cosmetics, and Martha Stewart. They are currently working on a mass-produced equivalent of their canvas rug.

Carmen Cheong
Lemongrass

Carmen Cheong studied product design at Temasek Polytechnique Singapore. She worked

Kelly Bortoluzzi & Kristin Ordahl
1-3, Bio (Bortoluzzi): Beth Schneckenberger
4: Patrick Rytikangas
Bio (Ordahl): Jeffrey Gibson

Laurene Leon Boym
1, Bio: Kristine Larsen
2-6: Boym Partners

Diana Brennan
1: Michel Brosset
2-7: Diana Brennan
Bio: Lola Greenwich

Nicolette Brunklaus
1, 3, 5, 7: Maarten van Houten
2, 4: Walter van Broekhuizen
6: Marc Gravemaker
Bio: Carry van der Maas

Louise Campbell
1-7: Erik Brahl
Bio: Hoang Sato

Jennifer Carpenter
1-6: Truck Product Architecture
Bio: Travis Huggett

Carmen Cheong
1: Oliver Schuh Palladium
2, 4, 5, Bio: Matteo Manduzio
3, 6: Jürgen Schwope

Jessica Corr
1-4, 6: Annie Schlechter
5: Jessica Corr
Bio: CYJO

Matali Crasset
1-3, 6, Bio: Patrick Gries
4, 5, 7: Uwe Spoering
8: Thomson Multimedia

Sophie Demenge
1, 2, 5: R+D Design
3, 4: Oeuf
Bio: Bruno Moyen

Han Feng
Han Feng New York

After graduating from the Zhejiang Academy of Fine Arts in Hangshou in 1985, Han Feng moved to New York. She began her career in fashion four years later with a collection of pleated scarves. Encouraged by the enthusiastic response, Feng opened her own company. Today, she continues to expand her horizons with seasonal ready-to-wear collections as well as ventures into furniture and home accessories. Feng is celebrated for her creative use of color and innovative fabric treatments and has made comfort, wearability, and beauty focal points of her collections.

Monica Förster

Monica Förster grew up in Dorotea, Lapland and graduated from Beckmans School of Design in Stockholm in 1995. She works as an independent designer as well as the international ambassador for Scandinavian design for the Swedish Foreign Ministry. Förster has been awarded the Excellent Swedish Design Award, among others, and has exhibited her work internationally. She has designed for David Design, Offecct, Skruf, E&Y, Nola Industrier AB, and Poltrona Frau.

Anki Gneib

Born in London in 1965, Anki Gneib received her degree from the University College of Art, Craft and Design in Stockholm. Since 1993, she has worked as an independent architect, and currently runs her own studio in Stockholm. A unique mark of her work involves the frequent use of symbolism. She has designed products for several companies including Arvesund, Asplund, Fogia, Interstop, Plan Ett, R.O.O.M., Offecct, and Skruf.

throughout Europe. Grawunder has held numerous solo exhibitions and collaborated with such companies as Flos, Boffi Salviati, JG Durand, Mikasa, and Christofle of France.

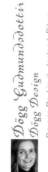

Camilla Groth

Camilla Groth was born in Stockholm in 1973. She received her BA in ceramics and glass at the University of Art and Design, Helsinki, Finland and her MA at the Royal College of Art, London. She has been a freelance designer working in both ceramic and glass throughout Europe and Japan. Some of her work is produced by Sarner Cristal, Switzerland and Master Craft, Japan. Groth is the recipient of numerous awards in both Sweden and Finland.

Dögg Gudmundsdóttir
Dögg Design

Born in Reykjavik, Iceland, Dögg Gudmundsdottir studied industrial design at the Istituto Europeo de Design in Milan and the Danmarks Designskole. Since completing her studies in 1998, Gudmundsdottir's work has been exhibited and published throughout Europe. She has designed for companies such as B-Sweden, Ligne Roset, Finn Frogne, and Elementi.

Anette Hermann
planA

Anette Hermann graduated from the Institute of Industrial Design at Denmark's Design School in Copenhagen. In 1997 she founded her own design firm, planA, in Copenhagen. Her international work ranges from interior and exhibit design to furniture, industrial design, fashion, lighting, and graphics. In 2003 her design Streol became part of the permanent collection of the

group, Liminal. After studying fashion design, Lande lived in Milan for many years and worked with the Japanese fashion designer Giuliano Fujiwara, where she was responsible for the women's wear collections. After earning her master's degree in industrial design in 1996, Lande's work has moved to low-tech products with a focus on human interactions.

Lily Latifi

In 1998 Franco-Iran an designer Lily Latifi received diplomas in tapestry and in textile design and print from the Ecole Supérieure des Arts Appliqués—Duperré in Paris. In 1999 she started her own company and, in 2001, she opened her first studio and showroom in Paris, showcasing textiles, accessories, and furniture. Latifi exhibits her work internationally and frequently receives private commissions as well as projects for haute couture houses.

Ilaria Marelli

Although she earned a degree in architecture and industrial design at the Politecnico di Milano, Ilaria Marelli extends her interests into photography, theater, marketing, and communications. From 1998 to 2003 she worked in brand management for Cappellini SpA. She has designed products for Zanotta SpA, Cappellini, Nemo Italianaluce-Cassina Group, Serralunga, Bosa Ceramiche, and Duepuntosette. In 2003 Marelli started her own design consultancy, in collaboration with Diana Eugeni, offering art direction and product design services for design-oriented companies. She is a professor of industrial design at the Politecnico di Milano and Scuola Politecnica di Design in Milan.

Ruby Metzner
Hivemindesign

Ruby Metzner graduated with a BFA in industrial design from the Rhode Island School of Design in 1995. She worked for designer Karim Rashid for several years and founded Hivemindesign with Sather Duke in 2000. Hivemindesign is a consulting firm and manufacturer of interiors, furniture, packaging, and products. Since its inception, it has been an active member of the growing Brooklyn design community.

Ana Mir
Emiliana Design Studio

Ana Mir Prieto was born in Valencia, Spain in 1969. She received a master's degree in industrial design at Central Saint Martins College of Art and Design in London and a bachelor of fine arts from the Universidad Politecnica de Valencia. Since founding Emiliana Design Studio in Barcelona with partner Emil Padrós, she has collaborated with a variety of different companies. Emiliana's work has been exhibited and recognized internationally. In 2000 Mir won first international prize in the Boeing Business Jet Interiors Competition held by Boeing and the Italia magazine Domus as well as the Barcelona City Award in Design.

Marre Moerel
Marre Moerel Design Studio

Born in the Netherlands, Marre Moerel studied fashion design in Rotterdam, received a degree in sculpture from Exeter in England, and graduated from the Royal College of Art with a master's degree in furniture design in 1991. She spent ten years in New York as a freelance designer and artist working with such acclaimed companies as Cappellini, Covo, Fiorucci, Offecct, Ozone, and Wilsonart. She currently resides in Madrid, Spain, where she runs her own design studio and gallery.

Trapholt Museum in Kolding, Denmark and the National Museum of Women in the Arts in Washington, D.C.

Dejana Kabiljo
Kabiljo Inc.

Born in Split, Croatia, Dejana Kabiljo received a master's degree in design from the Domus Academy in Milan and a degree in architecture from the University of Belgrade. She currently lives in Vienna, Austria where she founded her own professional practice and the production label, Kabiljo Inc., in 2001. Kabiljo has been involved with various museums in Vienna as an art director as well as exhibiting designer. Her piece SCRIBOman is included in the permanent collection of the MAK, Museum of Applied Arts/Contemporary Art, Vienna.

Defne Koz
Defne Koz Design Studio

Born in Turkey, Defne Koz received a master's degree in industrial design from Domus Academy in Milan, Italy and spent two years at Sottsass Associati before founding her eponymous Milan design consultancy in 1992. She has developed products for several companies, including Pirelli, Alessi, FontanaArte, Foscarini, Cappellini/Progetto Oggetto, Guzzini, Mobileffe, Liv.it, WMF, Sharp, Nissan, and Casio. Koz's innovative works have been exhibited in numerous venues, including the Kunstmuseum Dusseldorf, Ozore Gallery Tokyo, Triennale Milano, Galleria Posteria Milano, and Museo di Pietrarsa Naples.

Catherina Lande

Catherina Lande is an independent designer as well as the cofounder of the Nordic design

Lyn Godley

In 1984 Lyn Godley formed the product design firm Godley-Schwan with her partner Lloyd Schwan. Their furniture and lighting designs have been published and recognized internationally and are in the permanent collections of the Museum of Modern Art, New York, and the Museum of Art and Design, New York. Since 1998, Godley has worked independently as a designer and teaches product design at Parsons School of Design, New York.

Elisabetta Gonzo
(formerly of EG+AV)

Elisabetta Gonzo earned her degree in architecture at the University of Florence in 1988. She partnered with Alessandro Vicari in 1992 to form EG+AV, which developed many architecture and design projects. EG+AV has received a number of architectural awards, and some of their objects are part of permanent collection of the Musée des Arts Décoratifs in Paris. In 2001 Gonzo became a professor of design at the Accademia di Belle Arti of Catania. She currently has an independent practice in Milan, Italy.

Johanna Grawunder

After completing her studies in architecture at California Polytechnic State University in San Luis Obispo in 1985, spending her final year at the university's foreign campus in Florence, Johanna Grawunder joined Sottsass Associati in Milan, becoming a partner four years later. Grawunder has been behind some of the most prestigious architectural projects of the studio, such as Casa Wolf in Colorado and the Ernest Mourmans House in Belgium. Now based in San Francisco and Milan, she is currently working on her own architectural, interior, and lighting design projects and is a frequent lecturer

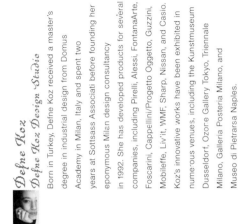

Dögg Gudmundsdottir
1–8: Sigurpóur Páll Sigurdsson
Bio: Dögg Gudmundsdottir

Anette Hermann
1–5, Bio: Erik Brahl

Dejana Kabiljo
1, 4: Dejana Kabiljo
2: Sergio Ephrem Raimondi
3, Bio: Lukas Hernfeld

Defne Koz
1: FontanaArte
2: Decorum
3: RSVP
4–6, 10: Defne Koz
7: Alessi
8: Nitoarredamenti Srl
9: Alparda
Bio: Cristiano Bottino

Catherina Lande
1–4: Johanna Rylander
5, 6: Magnor Glassverk AS
7: Chris Harrison
Bio: David Reid

Lily Latifi
1–3: Lily Latifi
Bio: Christophe Lepage

Ilaria Marelli
1: Zanotta SpA
2, Bio: Massimiliano Morlotti
3, 5: Cappellini
4: Bosa Ceramiche
6: Nemo Italianaluce, Cassina Group

Ruby Metzner
1–3: hivemindesign
Bio: Wouter Vandertol

Ana Mir
1, 6: Xavier Padrós
2: Emiliana Design Studio
3: Albert Font; courtesy of Nanimarquina
4, 5: Rafael Vargas
7: Enric Rovira
Bio: Jason Keith

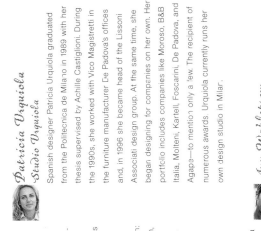

Patricia Urquiola
Studio Urquiola

Spanish designer Patricia Urquiola graduated from the Politecnica de Milano in 1989 with her thesis supervised by Achille Castiglioni. During the 1990s, she worked with Vico Magistretti in the furniture manufacturer De Padova's offices and, in 1996 she became head of the Lissoni Associati design group. At the same time, she began designing for companies on her own. Her portfolio includes companies like Moroso, B&B Italia, Molteni, Kartell, Foscarini, De Padova, and Agapé—to mention only a few. The recipient of numerous awards Urquiola currently runs her own design studio in Milan.

Ann Wahlstrom
Kosta Boda

Ann Wahlstrom has been experimenting with glass for more than twenty years. Born in Stockholm, Sweden, she has studied at the Glass School in Orrefors, Sweden, the Pilchuck Glass School, Rhode Island School of Design (under Dale Chihuly), and the University College of Arts, Craft and Design in Stockholm (under Paula Bartron and Bertil Vallier). She has exhibited her work in Sweden, Europe, the United States, and Australia and has worked with Kosta Boda since 1986.

Elizabeth Paige Smith

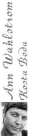

Raised in the Cayman Islands, Smith moved to the United States to attend the School of Fine Arts at Kansas University. After graduating in 1993, she settled in Los Angeles and established her design studio, where her projects include furniture design and interiors. Smith's work has been part of the Cooper-Hewitt, National Design Museum's 2002 exhibition Skin: Surface and Structure in Contemporary Design, and she has exhibited at the Museum of Contemporary Art at the Geffen Contemporary in Los Angeles.

Yuriko Takahashi

After graduating in industrial design from Chiba University's engineering department in 1991, Yuriko Takahashi worked at Matsushita Electronic Works Tokyo design department for five years. She then studied furniture design at the Royal Danish Academy of Fine Arts, and in 1999 she completed her degree at the Danmarks Designskole in Copenhagen. That same year she received the Bronze Prize at the International Furniture Design Fair in Asahikawa and Silver Prize in the Valencia International Furniture Design Competition.

Sarah Unruh

Sarah Unruh began working with textiles while studying furniture design at the Rhode Island School of Design. Upon graduating in 1999 with a bachelor of fine arts, she worked as a furniture designer for Dakota Jackson. In 2001 she began producing her own furniture and textile designs. She is currently working on a series of textiles for a large residential project, where she explores fabric as an architectural screen.

Lauren Moriarty

Lauren Moriarty studied multimedia textiles at Loughborough University United Kingdom, where her experiments in plastics and neoprene led her to develop three-dimensional fabric structures. Her lighting and textiles have been published extensively. Moriarty was the recipient of the Reebok Prize and the Dalsouple 100% Rubber Competition in 2002, and was short-listed for the 2002 Oxo/Peugeot Design Awards. She is currently earning her master's in industrial design from Central Saint Martins College of Art and Design in London.

Monica Nicoletti
Group Inc.

After establishing herself in both the Italian and the New York fashion markets, Monica Nicoletti began pursuing her fashion career as an independent design consultant. Her fashion sensibility has been an important contribution to the design success of Group Inc., in which she is a partner. When not experimenting in the area of soft goods for Group Inc., Nicoletti consults internationally with fashion companies and develops patterns and embellishments for a number of various product manufacturers.

Inga Sempé

In 1993 Inga Sempé received her degree from L'Ecole Nationale Supérieure de Création Industrielle—ENSCI/Les Ateliers in Paris. After graduation, she worked at the well-known design firms of George Sowden, Marc Newson, and Andrée Putman before forming her own design firm in 1999. She was awarded Grand Prix de la Création de Paris for design in 2002, and has produced works for Baccarat, Cappellini, Ghaadé, and Edra. In 2003 Sempé's first solo exhibition was held at the Musée des Arts Décoratifs in Paris.